The Basics of Foreign Exchange Markets

The Basics of Foreign Exchange Markets

A Monetary Systems Approach

William D. Gerdes

BEP BUSINESS EXPERT PRESS

The Basics of Foreign Exchange Markets: A Monetary Systems Approach

First published in 2015 by
Business Expert Press, LLC
222 East 46th Street, New York, NY 10017
www.businessexpertpress.com

ISBN-13: 978-1-60649-820-0 (paperback)
ISBN-13: 978-1-60649-821-7 (e-book)

Business Expert Press Economics Collection

Collection ISSN: 2163-761X (print)
Collection ISSN: 2163-7628 (electronic)

Cover and interior design by Exeter Premedia Services Private Ltd., Chennai, India

First edition: 2015

10 9 8 7 6 5 4 3 2 1

Printed in the United States of America.

To Harold and Joella Gerdes

Abstract

Foreign exchange markets are inextricably entwined with underlying monetary standards. Thus, they are treated conjointly. Four different exchange rate regimes are analyzed: (1) foreign exchange markets with commodity money; (2) foreign exchange markets with fiduciary money; (3) foreign exchange markets with fiat money—fixed exchange rates; and, (4) foreign exchange markets with fiat money—flexible exchange rates.

For the last eight decades, most countries have operated with fiat monies. For proponents of the fiat money standard, one of its desirable attributes is that it provides individual countries with considerable monetary autonomy. However, both analytics and experience indicate that this is not always the case. Whether a country has more monetary autonomy depends upon whether fiat money is paired with fixed exchange rates (regime 3) or flexible exchange rates (regime 4). More autonomy is possible with flexible exchange rates (regime 4). Such autonomy is largely possible because foreign exchange markets are allowed to accommodate the wide variations in national monetary policies. Under this regime, the purchasing power parity (PPP) theory of exchange rates assumes elevated importance in accounting for foreign exchange market adjustments.

Exchange rate regime 4 has been in place (in many countries) for more than four decades, and there are critics. Those who advocate scrapping this arrangement generally favor a return to either regime 2 or regime 3.

Keywords

central banking, commodity money, deflation, fiduciary money, fiat money, fixed exchange rates, flexible exchange rates, inflation, purchasing power parity

Contents

Preface

Let's learn about foreign exchange markets. These markets exist because there are many different monies used throughout the world. As a consequence, individuals often find it necessary to exchange monies for one another. Markets where such exchanges occur are foreign exchange markets.

Increased globalization of the world economy means that most people either participate directly or are indirectly impacted by activities in foreign exchange markets. This book provides the reader with an introduction to how these markets work. The approach is analytical, and draws upon the close relationship between foreign exchange markets and underlying monetary standards.

For the last four decades, most countries have employed a fiat money standard along with flexible exchange rates (or prices) in foreign exchange markets. The United States is among them, and considerable attention is paid to this particular institutional arrangement. Other institutional configurations such as fiat money with fixed exchange rates are analyzed. The adjustable-peg system of the International Monetary Fund (1944 to 1971) is a historical episode. The relationship between current monetary arrangements and the pre–World War II gold standard is also discussed.

This book would be perfect as an addendum to academic courses in money and banking, monetary theory, and international trade and finance. It is also useful as a source book on foreign exchange markets for business professionals.

Foreign Exchange Markets: A Monetary Systems Approach
William D. Gerdes

CHAPTER 1

Introduction

Foreign Exchange Markets: Street Smart

The equatorial mid-day humidity is stifling as I traverse, by foot, the city center of Dar es Salaam. As a newcomer to the country, I am marveling at the beehive of activity that is this city of nearly two million in a country that was once the German colony of Tanganyika, and later a part of the British Empire. Sidewalks are lined with card tables where vendors are actively hawking their wares, some with marketing skills that would put many westerners to shame.

I purchase a few German coins (dated 1916) that once circulated in the colonial days. Nearby is an entrepreneur selling cigarettes individually for those who cannot afford to buy a full pack. (I later find out that it is possible to purchase a cigarette by the puff.) A table with stacked copies of *The Economist* magazine catches my attention, but my interest wanes when I discover that the most recent one is nearly four years old. An attractive young woman dressed in a flowing green, pink, and white sari is selling tomatoes that are meticulously arranged in threesomes. A brief conversation reveals that she is a registered nurse, but can earn more by selling vegetables than by plying her nursing skills in a country that is starved for medical services.

The streets are crowded, and I continue to zigzag along sidewalks, occasionally glancing downward at cement slabs that are sometimes chipped or broken and generally showing much wear and tear since originally laid by the British. Suddenly, I bump shoulders with a young Tanzanian man with one hand cusped around his lips, who says just loudly enough for me to hear, "Change money, my friend?" As I looked back, I did not recognize this friend. However, he had certainly identified me as Mr. Hard Currency, and I had just been propositioned. For me, this was my informal entrance into a very vibrant corner of the foreign exchange market in this African country.

Although I declined this young man's offer, I soon learned much about the black market where U.S. dollars were exchanged for Tanzanian shillings. Indeed, expatriate faculty members were active participants, and some offered to assist me in obtaining a better rate for my U.S. dollars. University students in my classes approached me with the story that they needed to do a foreign exchange transaction with me to purchase an economics book priced in U.S. dollars. I was somewhat caught off guard when, on a visit to the U.S. embassy, a ranking embassy official cautioned me: Be certain to get a good rate for your dollars.

Six months later, I enjoy a very pleasant lunch in the open-aired restaurant atop the Kilimanjaro Hotel. We are surrounded by bougainvillea, now in full bloom. Perched before us in the middle of the Dar es Salaam harbor (possibly since Genesis) is the partially submerged ship, its bow forever pointed skyward. My waiter smiles broadly when I order Pepsi mbili (two Pepsis, right away). Once acclimated, life in the tropics can be utterly enchanting. Following my sumptuous meal, I pay and exit. The charge was $10 or $3.33, respectively, depending on whether one exchanges dollars with the government of Tanzania or in the black market.

As I enter my white Peugeot parked outside the hotel, two Tanzanian men dressed in business suits approach me. They identify themselves as police officers and state that they had a report that I had violated the foreign exchange control laws of Tanzania. Although my heart rate accelerates, I deny this allegation and suggest that they had the wrong individual.

When asked if I would mind coming down to the police station, I willingly comply. Outside the station, a third individual in full police uniform joins us. The three of them question me with the suggestion eventually made that we move under a nearby tree to avoid the heat. While the questions are rapid-fire, the officers thoughtfully remind me that one of their major concerns is to preserve my good name as a distinguished visitor in the country. After about 10 minutes of back-and-forth questions and answers, I more clearly comprehend the drift of their inquiries and pass the gentlemen 400 shillings. All depart.

Afterward, I walk down a nearby street attempting to process all that had transpired during the encounter. Suddenly, it hit me like a thunderbolt that, in all likelihood, at most only one of these three individuals was actually a police officer. In universities we refer to the payment I had just rendered as tuition—the remuneration offered for the privilege of learning.

These episodes in no way intimate that reading this book will help you become a more street-smart participant in foreign exchange markets. Quite the opposite, the intent is to make you more book-smart. This book provides you with a solid analytical foundation for understanding foreign exchange markets, and how they relate to underlying monetary standards. As you read, you will become better acquainted with important issues such as exchange-rate stability brought about by market forces, and how it differs from exchange rate stability occasioned by government price-fixing, what it means for a country to have a nonconvertible currency, how the central banks engage in the dirty float, and, yes, the nature of black markets in foreign exchange. If, along the way, you happen to become more street-smart, it could save you a few hundred shillings.

Foreign Exchange Markets: A Preview

Foreign exchange markets exist because there is not a single currency that is universally used to make exchanges. Consequently, market participants often find it necessary to exchange monies for one another. Markets where such exchanges occur are referred to as foreign exchange markets. For each pair of currencies, there is such a market and also a market price. The latter is known as the exchange rate.

The institutional arrangements surrounding foreign exchange markets are called exchange rate regimes. Each exchange rate regime is inextricably entwined with an underlying monetary standard. Hence, it makes sense to treat them conjointly. That is the approach adopted here, something apparent from the structure of the book.

In Chapter 2, the nature of money is discussed and the different monetary standards presented. The taxonomy of monies employed is one developed by the author,[1] and employed extensively in an earlier book in this series.[2] In the United States, we currently live in a world of fiat money that commenced with the imposition of that form of money by the F. D. Roosevelt administration in March 1933. The most prominent feature of this form of money is unrelenting inflation and the accompanying deterioration in the quality of money.

Chapter 3 is a short introduction to foreign exchange markets. How we account for international transactions is examined, with concepts such as the balance of trade and the balance of payments introduced. These are not novel concepts. We frequently encounter them through the news media. In its quest for the dramatic, the U.S. media is often prone to report that this country experienced a record balance of trade deficit the previous month. Notably missing is the corollary observation that, with flexible exchange rates, foreign exchange markets tend to clear and the *balance of payments* tends toward zero (in the limit) each month. When was the last time you recall accessing the evening news and encountering the lead story that "The balance of payments was zero again last month"? Me neither. Matters such as this one are addressed.

The following three chapters (4 through 6) provide a detailed discussion of various exchange rate regimes embedded in underlying monetary standards. Foreign exchange markets with commodity and fiduciary monies are the subject of Chapter 4. As *Homo sapiens*, most of our accumulated experience is with foreign exchange markets under these standards. However, as contemporaries we deviate from that pattern. Indeed, there are few of us who can claim any practical experience with foreign exchange markets under a commodity or fiduciary money standard.

Despite our inexperience, it is not difficult to make the case that we gain valuable insight through the study of how foreign exchange markets work under these monetary regimes. For one thing, it exposes us to the subtleties surrounding foreign exchange market activity when we operate with money that is both market-based and international in scope. A recent historical example is the gold standard.

Under fiduciary money regimes like the gold standard, foreign exchange markets are characterized by fixed exchange rates established through the activities of market traders. To understand adjustments in these markets, the price–specie flow mechanism of Scottish philosopher David Hume is a noteworthy contribution. Hume's analysis is an important reminder of how unfettered market traders are capable of adapting in complex environments that some would claim are only tractable when addressed through the medium of government.

These market dynamics aside, there is further reason to know something about how foreign exchange markets function under the gold standard. There are some among us who favor a return to a fiduciary monetary standard and the fixed exchange rates that they imply. While they are in the minority at present, any useful evaluation of their proposals presumes a working knowledge of how foreign exchange markets perform in this setting.

The 20th century witnessed a great upheaval in both the type of money used and the nature of activity in foreign exchange markets. Governments imposed fiat money regimes that, by their nature, involved national monies as opposed to more cosmopolitan international monies such as gold. This had enormous implications for those trading foreign exchange. Contrary to the previous experience, the exchange of monies for one another was now much more heavily impacted by national government policies. Given the dominance of fiat money regimes during the 20th and 21st centuries, the bulk of this book is devoted to the operations of foreign exchange markets under this monetary standard.

With fiat money, exchange rates can be either fixed or flexible. For approximately the first half of our experiment with fiat money, nearly all countries had fixed exchange rates; for the last half, most converted to flexible rates. In both instances, countries generally followed the economic lead of the United States. In the aftermath of World War II, this country had replaced the United Kingdom as the dominant economic power and major trading country in the international economy.

Chapter 5 is about fixed exchange rates in the world of fiat money. Such was the nature of monetary arrangements after World War II, when governments in both developed and less developed countries opted for fixed rates. Because the experiences of developed and less developed countries were, in many respects, dissimilar, they are chronicled separately in this chapter.

For developed countries, a new international organization, the International Monetary Fund (IMF), provided the framework for government price-fixing in foreign exchange markets. Fixed exchange rates were implemented through the medium of the market for gold. Because the previous monetary standard was built around gold, this new price-fixing scheme gave the appearance of continuity with the gold standard. Further exacerbating the confusion was the terminology used to describe the new arrangement: the gold-exchange standard. Moreover, both standards were characterized by fixed exchange rates. This led Milton Friedman to write a paper attempting to distinguish between a real gold standard and this one, which he referred to as a pseudo gold standard.[3]

Most less developed countries implemented fixed exchange rates by attaching their currencies to those of developed countries (such as the U.S. dollar, the British pound, or the French franc). What distinguished their experiences from those of the more developed countries was their greater reliance on seigniorage as a motive for money creation, much higher inflation rates, and the policies they enacted in response to balance of payment disequilibria, and particularly deficits.* As a result, numerous less developed countries operated with nonconvertible currencies and many had active black markets in foreign exchange.

Developed and less developed countries did share one very critical common experience when fixing exchange rates. It has to do with government price-fixing in markets more generally. In every such case, the relevant question ultimately becomes this one: What happens when the government-determined price is not the same as the price that would be generated based on the valuations of market traders (or the market price)? The inability of governments to resolve this valuation discrepancy is what led to the ultimate demise of the IMF's adjustable-peg system as well as government price-fixing schemes in less developed countries.

In this valuation tussle, markets most often trump governments (given enough time). Among the developed countries, the United States under President Richard M. Nixon was one of the first to bow to market forces. It was announced in a stunning speech delivered by President Nixon on August 15, 1971. The United States made foreign-held U.S. dollars inconvertible into gold at the central bank level (or closed the gold window), and also took the first step toward a flexible exchange rate

---

*Seigniorage is government revenue from money creation. This motive for creating money is much more prevalent in less developed countries. In these economies, the alternatives for financing government expenditures, such as income taxation or borrowing in financial markets, are often either not possible or much less productive. For a more detailed discussion of seigniorage, see Gerdes (2014).

for the U.S. dollar, something ultimately completed in 1973. All major trading countries and many less developed countries eventually followed the U.S. government's lead in the movement to flexible rates.

Chapter 6 covers fiat money with flexible exchange rates. For many countries, this exchange rate regime has now been in place for more than four decades. While exchange rates fluctuate upward and downward, central banks sometimes intervene in an attempt to override market valuations. This is known as the dirty float. When central banks do this collectively, it is called macroeconomic policy coordination. In a way, such foreign exchange market intervention is a hangover from the earlier period of government price-fixing in the decades from the 1940s into the 1970s. It suggests that governments are still not convinced that market traders are better at valuing foreign exchange than are governments.

The final chapter of the book is forward-looking. Of particular concern are proposals for replacing the system of flexible exchange rates now in place. The two major candidates are regressive in the sense that they propose returning to exchange rate regimes we experienced in the past. This makes their evaluation somewhat easier because we know something about them.

Extensions

The analysis in this book provides the reader with a general macro perspective on foreign exchange markets, and how they relate to underlying monetary standards. There was no attempt to be comprehensive. Not discussed, for example, are more recent nuances in the institutional arrangements for fixed and flexible exchange rate regimes. Currency boards, crawling pegs, and crawling bands are cases in point. Textbooks in international finance are a general source for an introductory discussion of these institutional arrangements.

Some familiarity with international institutions such as the IMF and the International Bank for Reconstruction and Development (World Bank) is a natural extension of this book. Such institutions were created in the aftermath of World War II to support the expansion of world trade. How these institutions originated and subsequently functioned is useful for understanding the evolution of postwar exchange rate regimes.

Chief among these institutions was the IMF, the institution that created and later monitored the adjustable-peg system for fixing exchange rates after the war. The structure of the IMF was hammered out at a conference in Bretton Woods, New Hampshire in 1944. The nature of those negotiations, and the views of major antagonists such as John Maynard Keynes and Harry Dexter White, was carefully chronicled in a recent book.[4] These negotiations were critical in defining the relative leadership roles for the United States and the United Kingdom in the postwar international economy.

The much-desired increase in post–World War II world trade did come to fruition. This was due, in part, to a concerted effort by the major trading nations to implement commercial policies that fostered an environment of greater international cooperation. The leadership role of the United States in this effort was crucial. Among the more influential commercial policies was the General Agreement on Tariffs and Trade (GATT). This set of agreements provided rules outlining acceptable government policies relating to trade, and also methods for resolving trade disputes between countries. At the end of the 20th century, the institutional framework for the GATT was superseded by the World Trade Organization (WTO). The history and major provisions of the GATT and the WTO are covered in standard textbooks in international economics and finance,[5] but more in-depth studies are also available.[6]

While this book provides a general framework for understanding foreign exchange markets, it is definitely not a practitioner's manual. A more detailed discussion of financial instruments, supporting banking institutions, and foreign exchange market activity is generally found in standard textbooks on international economics and international finance.[7] In these sources, you will encounter a wide variety of topics not covered in this book. Among them are the nature of forward markets and futures markets for foreign exchange, currency swaps, international banking facilities, and the various forms of foreign exchange risk.

CHAPTER 2

Money and Monetary Systems

Money and Our Living Standards

Markets are a spontaneous social institution where voluntary exchange occurs. They are one of our most important institutions, because of their enormous contribution to our material living standards. Every time voluntary exchange occurs, wealth is created. The wealth creation is not in the form of additional goods and services. Rather, it is in the form of additional *value* derived from those goods and services that are produced.

Voluntary exchange is predicated on valuation discrepancy. Individuals value things differently. In the process of exchange, each party gives up something they consider to have lesser value in exchange for something they perceive to have greater value. The consummation of an exchange results in the creation of value. Because the exchange is mutually beneficial, game-theorists refer to the activity as a positive-sum game, that is, social welfare increases.

Voluntary exchange is of two forms: direct exchange or indirect exchange. Barter is direct exchange, where goods and services are exchanged for other goods and services (G $\longleftrightarrow$ G). For example, individual A possesses wheat but would like to exchange some of that wheat for a baseball glove. That individual must find another (individual B) who has a baseball glove he or she is willing to exchange for some wheat. If there are two such individuals, and they agree on a rate of exchange (e.g., 12 bushels of wheat for one glove), an exchange occurs.

Exchange involving the use of money is called indirect exchange. Rather than a direct exchange of goods as in barter, goods are exchanged for an intermediate good (money), which is then exchanged for other goods and services (G → M → G). At first, this appears to be less efficient as it requires an extra transaction. That cannot be the case. If the use of money were less efficient, individuals would prefer barter and the use of money would dwindle. In practice that generally is not true. Nearly all transactions that we observe involve the use of money.

Because of the indirect nature of the exchanges involving money, money is typically defined as any *generally* accepted medium of exchange.[1] While monies in use today are often associated with governments, it is important to note that money is not the product of government. The use of money predates all modern forms of government. Rather, money is a *behavioral* phenomenon in the sense that money is whatever individuals opt to use as an exchange medium.[2]

The concept of money is necessarily dynamic because what people do select for use as money varies by time and place. In virtually every culture, money in use today differs from that used in the past. Moreover, at any point in time, one can observe different forms of money used in different locations. Money used for purchases in an African village market is different from money used to settle bond transactions in the world's major money centers. Both are different from that used in an isolated subculture in Papua New Guinea.

Two important considerations related to the use of money are: (1) its general dominance over barter as a form of exchange and (2) the enormous contribution that money makes to our material living standards. These are discussed in the same order.

Economists introduce the concept of transactions costs to explain the dominance of monetary over barter transactions. These costs are the resources that individuals must invest to participate in an exchange. They are of three principal types: (1) information costs, (2) transportation costs, and (3) storage costs.

Information is not a free good. If it were, quantities and offer prices for all goods and services would be known by everyone. Since a single individual does not possess all this information, resources frequently must be invested to acquire additional information prior to an exchange. In the barter example given earlier, the individual with wheat must use resources to seek out an individual with a baseball glove. Once a generally accepted exchange medium is in use, it generally requires fewer resources to sell the wheat for money, and to use the money to purchase a baseball glove. With fewer resources expended, the transactions costs of exchange are reduced.

A second type of transactions costs is transportation costs. Parties to an exchange must transport those items to be exchanged. Most monies are relatively easy to transport, and one can do so at a relatively low cost. It is not very difficult, for example, to carry one's wallet or checkbook to the market. In a barter economy, by contrast, individuals often must transport commodities (such as wheat) to the market at considerably higher cost. Thus, use of money normally reduces transactions costs due to its relative ease of transport.

Finally, storage costs arise because of the necessity of storing items that serve as an exchange medium. Like other transactions costs, they normally cannot be avoided. In the case of barter, storage costs tend to be relatively high because of the greater number of commodities one must inventory, and because some of them deteriorate while in storage. An example of the latter is grain spoilage that occurs during its holding period. In contrast to barter, money is generally less costly to store although there are storage costs here too. Today, they often assume the form of either service fees charged by banks, or the erosion in the purchasing power of money (PPM) due to inflation.

The contribution that money makes to our material well-being is related to the transactions costs of exchange. As transactions costs incurred when using money are often considerably lower than the transactions costs involved when engaging in barter transactions, the sentiment is that the use of money greatly increases the total number of voluntary exchanges that occur. Given that every voluntary exchange is wealth enhancing, the use of money contributes in a major way to improvements in our living standards.

Secondary Functions of Money

Money is defined in terms of its primary function. It serves as a medium of exchange. However, it also performs other functions: as a store of value, unit of account, and standard of deferred payment. These are referred to as the secondary functions of money because they generally derive from money's use as a medium of exchange.

The store of value function of money refers to its use as a vehicle for transferring purchasing power through time. It performs this function even when it is held for relatively short periods of time as an exchange medium. However, it also serves as a store of value when it is held for longer periods as a form of accumulated wealth.

Money is not unique in performing this function. Individuals hold various types of nonmonetary financial assets such as time and savings deposits at banks, government and corporate bonds, and equities (or ownership in private corporations). In addition, wealth is accumulated in the form of real assets, for example, land, buildings, jewelry, and paintings. Despite these alternative forms of holding wealth, nearly all individuals hold a portion of their wealth in the form of money. A major reason for doing so is that money is the most liquid of assets. That is, it gives its holder immediate access to markets.

Money also serves as a unit of account (or measure of value). In a monetary economy, the exchange value of all goods and services are quoted in terms of money, and comparative valuations are made by referring to monetary values of objects. If a watch sells for $100 and a tennis racquet for $200, we say that the tennis racquet is twice as valuable as the watch. If money were not used in this way, it would be much more difficult to make relative comparisons and transactions costs would increase significantly.

A final function of money is that it is customary to write loan contacts in terms of money. In this function, money is referred to as a standard of deferred payment. It is not necessary that money serve this function. It is possible, for example, to write a loan contract in which the proceeds of the loan (and subsequent repayment) are payable in corn, wheat, or any other commodity. However, it is unlikely that both parties to a loan contract would find one of these commodities agreeable. As a consequence, virtually all credit contracts involve payment in money.

The Value of Money

One of the functions of money is that it serves as a unit of account. Our valuation of things is expressed in terms of how many units of money we are willing to exchange for them. The unit of account function does not work, however, when it comes to valuing money. It is not fruitful to express the value of money in terms of itself. Doing so always yields the trivial value of one. The number of U.S. dollars that exchanges for one unit of U.S. money ($1) is precisely one. Likewise, the number of British pounds that exchanges for one unit of U.K. money (one pound) is also one.

As an alternative, it is customary to express the value of money in terms of how it exchanges against all other things. Consequently, the exchange value of money, or the PPM, works out to be the reciprocal of the average price (P) of things other than money. (P is sometimes referred to as the price level.)

$$PPM = 1/P, \tag{2.1}$$

where $P = (\overline{P_1, P_2, P_3, \dots, P_n})$.

Because valuation is a subjective phenomenon, individuals can and do change their minds about the value of things. This is true for money, too. Consequently, the value of money is subject to continuous variation. When consumers do revalue money, its value can increase or decrease.

Money loses value when consumers value it less in relation to goods and services. When they are willing to spend, on average, more units of money for goods and services, the result is an increase in the price level (P). Situations where P increases (and the PPM decreases) are known as inflation.

Deflation occurs when consumers value money more relative to goods and services. Consumers are now willing to exchange fewer units of money, on average, for goods and services. In such situations, the average price of goods and services (P) falls, and the PPM increases.

Types of Monetary Systems

There are three general types of monetary systems: commodity, fiduciary, and fiat.[3] Exhibit 2.1 summarizes the differences among them. The major identifying characteristics are (1) whether money has the same value when used for monetary and nonmonetary purposes and (2) whether money is convertible into a specified amount of commodity money on demand (at financial institutions).

Nearly all of our accumulated monetary experience is with commodity money. Fiduciary elements were introduced only in recent centuries,

Exhibit 2.1

Characteristics of different monies

Type of money	Equivalent value in monetary and nonmonetary use	Greater value in monetary use	Convertibility option
Commodity	X		
Fiduciary		X	X
Fiat		X	

and it was not until the 20th century that nearly every society converted to the use of fiat money. From a broad historical perspective, the type of money used by nearly everyone today is a relatively recent phenomenon.

Commodity Money

Commodity money has an important identifying characteristic: Its value when used for monetary purposes tends toward *equivalency* with its value when used for nonmonetary purposes. Note that this type of money is defined in terms of subjective value considerations and not any characteristic of the underlying commodity involved. It is the value of money in its potential alternative uses that is critical.

Nonmonetary uses of money occur when money is used for some purpose other than as money. This may or may not involve a transformation of money's constituent commodity. For example, gold coins can be used as paper weights or for various decorative purposes. Alternatively, these coins could be melted down and the gold used to make bracelets or any other form of jewelry. Use of money for such nonmonetary purposes is common throughout the history of commodity money systems, whether the particular object serving as money is cattle, wampum, sea shells, tobacco, bronze, iron, gold, or sliver.

The tendency for money to have equal value in monetary and nonmonetary uses is brought about through the exchange activities of individual consumers. The process is one of subjective value arbitrage. When gold is used as money, it is in the self-interest of each consumer to substitute holdings of money balances (gold coins) and nonmonetary gold (jewelry) for one another until the value of gold in these alternative uses is equal (at the margin). If gold has a greater marginal value when used as money, jewelry is melted down and the money supply increases. Alternatively, if gold has greater marginal value when used as jewelry, gold coins are melted down and the money supply falls. Valuation arbitrage ceases and the money supply stabilizes when, for the consumer, money has equal value in monetary and nonmonetary uses.

Fiduciary Money

Fiduciary money differs from commodity money in two respects. First, its value (at the margin) when used for monetary purposes exceeds its value (at the margin) when used for nonmonetary purposes. For that reason, one generally does not observe individuals using fiduciary money for nonmonetary purposes.

Second, fiduciary money has a convertibility option. The convertibility option is typically a (paper) contract to pay a specified amount of commodity money on demand. For example, under the gold standard, the statement "Pay to the Bearer on Demand: Twenty Dollars" was printed on a $20 bill. This bank note had a convertibility option. When it was presented to the issuer, the bank was obliged to pay the bearer (on demand) $20 in monetary gold.

The convertibility option is an important attribute in two respects. First, it was critical for the acceptance of early forms of fiduciary money and, hence, the evolution of this type of money. When commodity money was the common exchange medium, it is difficult to imagine a scenario where individuals would willingly have accepted paper money (with no convertibility option). Indeed, proposing that one do so would likely have met with considerable derision.

What made paper (or fiduciary) money acceptable in exchange *was* the convertibility option. After all, the first property of this money is that it has greater value when used as money than when used for nonmonetary purposes. The convertibility option helps the consumer overcome this liability by providing them with a valuable hedge. They can always convert fiduciary money into commodity money, which does tend to have equivalent value in nonmonetary usage.

Second, the convertibility option limits the total quantity of fiduciary money in circulation. This is especially important once governments commandeer control over money. The issue of more and more fiduciary money reduces the overall ratio of commodity money to fiduciary money. This ratio cannot fall indefinitely because the stability of the financial system eventually is jeopardized. If enough users of fiduciary money become concerned that they will be unable to convert their fiduciary money into commodity money on demand, the potential for a bank run arises (i.e., a large-scale withdrawal of commodity money from banks). This threat of a potential collapse of the financial system discourages further expansion of fiduciary money.

We do not know the origins of fiduciary money but it is reasonable to infer that it was a spontaneous market development. After all, its use offers the consumer the opportunity to reduce transactions costs associated with making exchanges. One popular hypothesis integrates the development of fiduciary money with the activities of early goldsmiths.

In the evolution of money as an exchange medium, business enterprises commenced to provide the service of safekeeping commodity money for those who did not wish to keep their accumulated money holdings in their homes. Individuals would bring monetary gold to the business for storage and receive a (paper) receipt acknowledging the deposit. Businesses would charge a small fee for this service, or might possibility do it without charge for a friend or regular business customer. Most likely, those were goldsmiths who provided this service because it was necessary for them to secure inventories of gold as a normal part of their business activity. It also is quite probable that banking originated in this manner, as those goldsmiths were performing what is now called the depository function of banks. Thus, it is common to refer to goldsmiths performing this function as early bankers.

When an individual wanted to make a purchase, he or she would go to the goldsmith, withdraw gold coins, and exchange them for the item of interest. In a village or small town, it is quite possible that the individual receiving the gold coins would take them to the same goldsmith for deposit. Transactions costs were lower if the first individual simply transferred ownership of the deposit (by offering the deposit receipt issued by the goldsmith) to the second individual. Doing so saved both a trip to the goldsmith. Once this started to happen, what people were using as an exchange medium had changed. They now were making purchases with commodity money and with paper claims on this money. The paper claims were serving as fiduciary money.

Although people often identify it as a form of commodity money, the gold standard of the 19th and early 20th centuries is a prime example of fiduciary money. The confusion exists because all fiduciary monetary systems are hybrid arrangements. Commodity money in the form of gold coins and fiduciary money that was convertible into commodity money on demand were both employed as exchange media.

Fiat Money

Fiat money has two distinctive features. Like fiduciary money, it has the property that its value when used as money exceeds its value when used for nonmonetary purposes.[4] The difference is the convertibility option. Fiduciary money is convertible (at issuing institutions) into commodity money on demand; fiat money is not.

This distinction is critical for understanding the origins of fiat money. Unlike commodity and fiduciary monies, fiat money was not a spontaneous market development. It did not result from the efforts of market participants to lower their transactions costs. Instead, it came about through the efforts of governments to gain greater control over money. Already active in the monetary process, 20th-century governments imposed fiat money arrangements by confiscating monetary gold and invoking laws abrogating the convertibility option associated with fiduciary money.

However, by now most individuals were quite accustomed to using paper money to effectuate exchanges. Under the fiduciary money standard, they frequently did so in order to reduce their transactions costs. Thus, movement to the fiat money standard did not require a significant modification of their behavior. Nonetheless, consumers did have a preference for fiduciary money.[5] That meant that governments (like the U.S. government) found it necessary to impose laws making it illegal for individuals to hold commodity money to discourage further usage.[6]

Fiat Money and the Age of Inflation

Historical data indicate that fluctuations in the value of money are intimately related to the type of monetary system in use. That has certainly been true for the United States. Figure 2.1 shows the price level for the U.S. economy for the period from the Revolutionary War until 2013. The 153-year period from 1780 to 1933 was predominately one where commodity and fiduciary monies were employed. While prices of goods and services changed more or less continuously, as one might expect, the period was generally one of long-run price stability. The average price of goods and services in 1933 was about the same as it was in 1780—only about 6 percent lower. The long-run value of money was virtually stable.

This long-run stability in the value of money was not a historical accident. Economic analysis suggests that we are likely to experience greater long-run price stability if we use commodity or fiduciary money rather than fiat money. The reason is that market forces are present that tend to bring about long-run price stability with commodity or fiduciary money. There are no comparable market forces under a fiat money standard.

Consider the case of commodity money. An increase in the general price level is equivalent to a decline in the exchange value of money relative to goods and services. Because relative prices have moved in favor of goods and services, and against money, economic incentives exist for

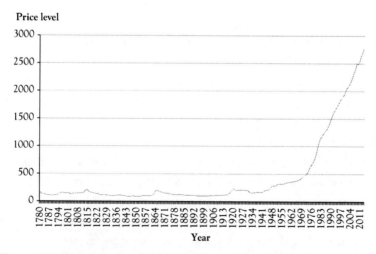

Figure 2.1 The price level: United States, 1780–2013

Source: David and Solar (1977) and U.S. Department of Labor (2014)

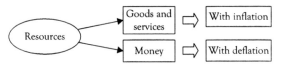

Figure 2.2 Changes in the value of money and resource reallocation

producers to employ more resources in the production of goods and services and fewer in the production of commodity money. The resulting
reallocation of resources is shown in Figure 2.2. The decline in the production of money, and increase in the production of goods and services,
combine to dampen (and ultimately terminate) the upward pressure on
the average price.

Those same market forces also render deflation self-limiting. With
a falling price level, money is gaining exchange value relative to goods
and services. Market incentives now encourage the allocation of more
resources for the production of money and fewer for the production of
goods and services. This reallocation or resources is shown in Figure 2.2.

For example, under the gold standard, deflation gives producers
of gold the incentive to devote more resources to the discovery of new
sources of that commodity. Those same producers may also invest additional resources to develop new technologies that improve mining and
refining techniques in the gold mining industry. The longer-term results
of such activities are an increase in the production of gold, an increase
in the quantity of commodity money, and an eventual end of deflation.

The cogency of these arguments is unaffected with the introduction
of fiduciary money. The major difference is that, in the short run, it is
now possible for governments (or banks) to adjust the quantity of fiduciary money and temporarily neutralize the effect of movements in relative prices on the production of commodity money. That is not possible,
however, in the long run.

With inflation, what limits the continued issue of fiduciary money is
the convertibility option. The introduction of more and more fiduciary
money to offset the declining production of commodity money occasions a
rise in the ratio of fiduciary money to commodity money. This cannot occur
indefinitely because the stability of the financial system eventually is jeopardized. If enough users of fiduciary money become concerned that they
will be unable to convert their fiduciary money into commodity money on

demand, the potential for a bank run arises (i.e., a large-scale withdrawal of commodity money from banks). This threat discourages the introduction of additional fiduciary money and inflation ultimately subsides.[7]

These automatic forces resulting in long-run price stability with commodity or fiduciary money are not present under a fiat money standard. The United States experience with fiat money affirms this. Through an executive order, President Franklin D. Roosevelt forced the country off the gold standard in March 1933. Previously, market forces, manifested in the form of the convertibility option, constrained how much fiduciary money the U.S. government could print. Elimination of the convertibility option removed that constraint.

Figure 2.1 shows the impact on the price level in the United States. The Federal Reserve was now in a position to print any amount of fiat money it chose. The revealed preference of the Federal Reserve was to continuously augment the quantity of fiat money. The consequence was secular inflation. Under the Federal Reserve's watch, the U.S. dollar lost approximately 94 percent of its purchasing power from 1933 to 2013.

The 20th-century implementation of the fiat money standard was international in scope. So, too, was the secular inflation. Nearly all countries experienced depreciation in the value of their currencies in excess of what happened in the United States. For many, the depreciation was greater than 99 percent. Appropriately, the world of fiat money has been dubbed the age of inflation.

Monetary Standards and Foreign Exchange Markets

Foreign exchange markets are markets where different monies are exchanged for one another. The institutional arrangements surrounding these markets are known as exchange rate regimes. Four such regimes are discussed in this book. Invariably, exchange rate regimes are paired with monetary standards. The remainder of this book explores the four different exchange rate regimes and their accompanying monetary standards. They are (1) foreign exchange markets with commodity money; (2) foreign exchange markets with fiduciary money; (3) foreign exchange markets with fiat money (fixed exchange rates); and (4) foreign exchange markets with fiat money (flexible exchange rates).

CHAPTER 3

Foreign Exchange Markets

Exchange Rate Regimes

There is not a single money that is used globally. As a consequence, it is necessary to exchange one money for another when engaging in international transactions. Markets where such exchanges occur are foreign exchange markets. Prices in these markets are called exchange rates, and there exists an exchange rate for each pair of currencies.[1]

Because exchanges in these markets involve trading one unit of account for another, it is customary to quote the price in terms of each of the currencies involved. For example, in the market where U.S. dollars and British pounds are exchanged, one can refer to the price of pounds in terms of dollars ($2 = 1£). Alternatively, one can express the same exchange rate as the price of dollars in terms of British pounds, that is, 0.50£ = $1. In this respect, foreign exchange markets differ from other markets where typically only one of the two items exchanged is money (and thus a unit of account). One speaks of the price of a hat as $50, but not the price of a dollar as 1/50 of a hat.

The degree of flexibility in exchange rates is dependent upon the type of money in use and government policies toward exchange rates. The various possibilities are outlined in Exhibit 3.1. The types of money are those discussed in Chapter 2. Note that traders, or buyers and sellers in the private sector, determine the exchange rate in all cases but one. Government price-fixing for foreign exchange becomes a potential issue with the use of fiat money. Prior to examining different exchange rate regimes, a brief discussion of the accounting for international exchanges is undertaken.

Exhibit 3.1 Exchange rate regimes with different types of money

Type of money	Exchange rate	Source of pricing
Commodity	Fixed	Traders
Fiduciary	Fixed	Traders
Fiat	Flexible	Traders
Fiat	Fixed	Government

Accounting for International Transactions

Because there are two sides to every transaction, the total value of things sold (S) by residents of a country must equal the total value of things bought (B) by those residents.[2] In this very general sense, the balance of exchanges for residents of any country will always be in balance.

$$S \equiv B \qquad (3.1)$$

The items exchanged are classified into three groups: goods and services (G), nonmonetary financial instruments (NM), or money (M). NM is sometimes referred to as stocks and bonds. Identity 3.1 can now be rewritten by incorporating this taxonomy.

$$(G + NM + M)_S = (G + NM + M)_B \qquad (3.2)$$

This identity does not generally hold if one considers proper subsets of total transactions. When accounting for international transactions, it often is of interest to compare the value of goods and services sold and goods and services purchased by residents of a particular country. That difference, $G_S - G_B$, is commonly referred to as the balance of trade (BOT) for the country. In Exhibit 3.2, Country A has a positive trade balance of 40 since its exports of goods and services exceed its imports by that amount. Given that the overall balance of exchanges must balance, Country A must have a balance of financial instruments deficit. That is, it must import 40 more in financial instruments (NM + M) than it exports. In this case, the BOT surplus is financed by a net importation of money balances from abroad.[3]

By contrast, Countries B and C have a BOT deficit of 40. That is, the value of exports minus the value of imports of goods and services is equal to −40 for both countries. These countries finance their trade deficits differently. Country B finances its deficit by exporting money balances (M). Country C finances its deficit with a balance of nonmonetary financial instruments (NM) surplus. That is, Country C is a net exporter of stocks and bonds and, thus, does not (in the net) ship money balances abroad.

The balance of payments (BOP) position of a country is another measure of international financial flows. This figure is derived by subtracting the total value of a country's imports of both goods and services (G) and nonmonetary financial instruments (NM) from its exports of the same.

Exhibit 3.2

Balance of trade and payments

Country A			
	S	B	Difference (S – B)
(G) Goods and services	140	100	40
(NM) Nonmonetary financial instruments	60	60	0
(M) Money	20	60	–40
Total	220	220	0

Country B			
	S	B	Difference (S – B)
(G) Goods and services	100	140	–40
(NM) Nonmonetary financial instruments	60	60	0
(M) Money	60	20	40
Total	220	220	0

Country C			
	S	B	Difference (S – B)
(G) Goods and services	100	140	–40
(NM) Nonmonetary financial instruments	80	40	40
(M) Money	40	40	0
Total	220	220	0

For this measure, Country A has a BOP surplus (+40). Because it sells 40 more of G and NM than it purchases, it is a net importer of money balances in the amount of 40. By contrast, Country B is a net exporter of money balances because it has a BOP deficit for the period. The BOP for Country C is in balance. Its exportation of money balances to finance overseas purchases of G and NM is exactly offset by its importation of money balances that results from international sales of G and NM.

It should be clear by now that an imbalance of payments between countries gives rise to monetary shipments from the deficit country to the surplus country. Recipients of these money balances in surplus countries are owners of money balances denominated in a foreign currency. Foreign money balances generally flow to the central bank of the surplus country as their owners exchange them for domestic money at commercial banks. Commercial banks, in turn, exchange them for domestic money at the central bank. If the central bank of the surplus country chooses not to hold these money balances as international reserves, it can redeem them (for domestic money) at central banks of deficit countries. Central banks in these deficit countries lose foreign exchange reserves as a consequence of this repatriation of money balances shipped overseas.

Digression on the U.S. Balance of Trade Deficit

The U.S. BOT deficit, which has persisted for more than three decades, has received much attention. It is not uncommon for the news media to report (with dramatic undertones) that the U.S. trade deficit reached a record level the previous month. Many observers (including some economists) consider such deficits a significant problem that requires fixing—presumably by the government.

While there is much drama in reporting record U.S. trade deficits, there generally is no mention of the U.S. balance of payments (BOP) position. The reason is that the BOP tends toward zero each month. That has been the case since the United States adopted flexible exchange rates in the early 1970s. As is discussed in Chapter 6, with a flexible exchange rate, the foreign exchange market clears and the BOP position goes to zero. There is, as a result, no BOP problem to report.

With a BOT deficit and a (proximate) zero BOP position, the aggregate accounting position for the United States is like that of Country C in Exhibit 3.2. In the aggregate, individuals in the United States are purchasing more goods and services from overseas sources than U.S. business are selling to those in other countries. This BOT deficit is financed by a balance of nonmonetary financial instruments (NM) surplus. That is, we are collectively financing our net importation of goods and services by selling economic agents in foreign countries more stocks and bonds than we are purchasing from them.

From a market-oriented perspective, it makes little sense to describe this situation as a problem. The foreign exchange market is clearing, so there is no impending crisis as there sometimes is when government sets the price of foreign exchange. The millions of economic agents using the foreign exchange market have selected that combination of goods, services, stocks, and bonds that best serve their particular needs. The fact that, collectively, these choices have resulted in a United States BOT deficit simply means that individuals living overseas generally prefer our stocks and bonds to our goods and services.

The relative attractiveness of our stocks and bonds is not something to necessarily bemoan. It partially reflects the fact that the United States is a country that is both politically stable and economically free—at least in a relative sense. As a consequence, many overseas investors feel comfortable buying financial instruments in this country. If this situation were to change and the United States had a military dictatorship with less political and economic freedom, it is quite likely that our negative trade balance would vanish.

CHAPTER 4

Foreign Exchange Markets With Commodity and Fiduciary Monies

Commodity Money

Commodity money is money that, at the margin, has equivalent value whether used for monetary or nonmonetary purposes. For the sake of exposition, assume that the money under consideration is gold. Assume, as well, that there are no fiduciary elements present in the system. This is a pure gold standard, with economic agents free to export and import gold.

Under such an arrangement, a given quantity of monetary gold should exchange for an equivalent amount of monetary gold. That is the basis for fixed exchange rates with a commodity money standard. In the following example, both the United States and the United Kingdom are on the gold standard. The basic monetary unit in the United States is called the dollar. Each dollar, when minted as a coin, contains 1/20th of an ounce of gold. Likewise, people in the United Kingdom are using gold for money. However, the basic monetary unit in this country is called the pound, which contains 1/10th of an ounce of gold. The fixed exchange rate between the dollar and the pound under this arrangement is $2 = 1£. Only at this exchange rate will equivalent amounts of gold be exchanged for one another. Two U.S. dollars contain 1/10th ounce of gold, which is the exact gold content of one British pound.

Fixed exchange rates with commodity money are not the consequence of government dictum, nor are they something handed down by a deity. Instead, they result from the activities of market traders. Any deviation from this fixed rate of exchange will provide profit opportunities for traders, and their arbitrage activities will restore the 2:1 rate of exchange.[1]

Consider, for example, what would happen if the market price of 1£ were $4 instead of $2. At this exchange rate, 1/5th of an ounce of gold ($4) is exchanging for 1/10th of an ounce of gold (1£). The U.S. dollar is undervalued (relative to its commodity content); the British pound, overvalued. It does not require an advanced degree in economics to devise a strategy to profit from this situation: sell the overvalued currency and buy the undervalued one.

In this case, market traders will sell British pounds and buy U.S. dollars in the foreign exchange market. The $4 acquired for each pound sacrificed is taken to the British mint. When melted down, the $4 produces 1/5th ounce of gold which is then minted into 2£. The one pound initially sold in the foreign exchange market has now generated 2£ for the market trader. The 2£ acquired from the mint are taken back to the foreign exchange market and again exchanged for U.S. dollars. Such arbitrage activity increases the supply of the overvalued currency and increases the demand for the undervalued currency. It continues until the 2:1 exchange rate is restored.

The Hume Price-Specie Flow Mechanism: Commodity Money

If commodity money standards give rise to a fixed exchange rate for each pair of currencies, what assurance do we have that any given fixed exchange rate will be a market clearing one? That is, how do we know that the quantity demanded will exactly equal quantity supplied at that fixed price?

Figure 4.1 shows the market for the U.S. dollar in terms of British pounds. The vertical axis is the price of dollars in terms of pounds and the horizontal axis is the quantity of dollars. Economic agents demanding dollars in this market are supplying pounds. They do so to purchase U.S. goods and services (G) and nonmonetary financial instruments (NM). Similarly, those supplying dollars are demanding pounds which positions them to purchase goods, services, and nonmonetary financial instruments denominated in U.K. pounds.

In Figure 4.1, the fixed price of 0.5 pound per dollar is not a market clearing one. There is an excess supply of dollars in the amount of $S_1 - D_1$.

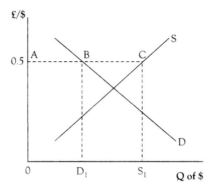

Figure 4.1 *Market for U.S. dollars*

An excess supply of dollars is equivalent to saying that the United States is running a balance of payments (BOP) deficit with the United Kingdom. The size of the deficit is equal to the rectangle D_1BCS_1.

Rectangle $0ACS_1$ represents the total value (expressed in pounds) of dollars supplied in order to import British goods and services and nonmonetary financial instruments. It is the price of dollars ($0.5£/\$$) times the quantity of dollars supplied (S_1). The total value (expressed in £) of U.S. exports of goods and services and nonmonetary financial instruments corresponds to the rectangle $0ABD_1$. The U.S. BOP deficit is the difference in these two rectangles.

The U.S. deficit is financed by the shipment of money balances to the United Kingdom. This raises a critical question. If individuals in the United States are free to export and import money balances, what will keep them from shipping the country's entire money stock to the United Kingdom? If this were to happen, there would be no money left in the United States for conducting business.

Such a prospect would appear to justify government intervention in the form of exchange controls to limit the ability of its citizens to export money. These concerns were the basis for mercantilist policies of European monarchies, particularly in the 17th and 18th centuries. A stated objective of those policies was, indeed, to limit the outflow of a country's commodity money, that is, to keep the money at home.

Economists credit British philosopher David Hume with developing the analysis that undermined such mercantilist thought and gave impetus to the free trade movement in 18th- and 19th-century Europe. According to Hume,[1] government intervention in foreign exchange markets is unnecessary. Automatic forces of the market, in the absence of any government intrusion, will bring about equilibrium in foreign exchange markets. The equilibration process is the result of a reallocation of the world's money supply from BOP deficit countries to surplus countries.

The shipment of money balances from the United States to the United Kingdom in the previous example changes the money stock in each country. The quantity of money now is lower in the United States (the deficit country) and higher in the United Kingdom (the surplus country). The spending of additional money balances in the United Kingdom results in higher prices in that country. Reduced spending in the United States (due to a lower money supply) causes prices to fall in that country.[2] With a fixed exchange rate, relative prices now have changed in the two countries. U.S. goods are now more price-competitive (relative to British goods) than they were before.

Effects of these relative-price changes on the foreign exchange market are shown in Figure 4.2. An increased number of individuals holding pounds now want to make purchases in the United States. Thus, the demand curve for dollars shifts to the right (from D to D′). On the other hand, fewer individuals in the United States are interested in purchasing goods from the United Kingdom. This causes the supply curve for dollars to shift to the left (from S to S′).

The world money stock is reallocated until the U.S. BOP deficit disappears (simultaneously with the British surplus). At the fixed exchange rate of 0.5£ = $1, the quantity of dollars demanded (D_2) now is exactly equal to the quantity supplied (S_2). All of these changes occur without government intervention in the foreign exchange market, and without any change in the exchange rate. The entire adjustment is in the form of changes in both the prices of goods and services and nominal incomes in the two countries.

This compelling argument is now called the Hume price-specie flow mechanism. Adjustments under the Hume mechanism are summarized

---

[1]Eugene Rotwein (ed.). David Hume: Writings on Economics. Madison, WI: University of Wisconsin Press, 1970.

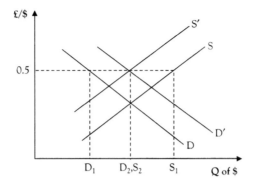

Figure 4.2 Market for U.S. dollars

Notes: £ = British pound, D = demand, S = supply

Exhibit 4.1

Adjustments under the Hume mechanism

Deficit country:	$-\Delta M$	$\rightarrow$	$-\Delta P$	$\rightarrow$	reduction in BOP deficit
Surplus country:	$+\Delta M$	$\rightarrow$	$+\Delta P$	$\rightarrow$	reduction in BOP surplus

in Exhibit 4.1. It might be better labeled the Hume specie-flow price mechanism. Changes in money (specie-flow) ultimately bring about the changes in prices that are necessary to clear the foreign exchange market.

The Hume Price-Specie Flow Mechanism: Fiduciary Money

When we introduce fiduciary money, Hume's argument is still valid. However, the situation now is different because governments (as issuers of fiduciary money) can, in the short-run, either hasten or retard the adjustment mechanism of Hume.

Governments can hasten the adjustment process in the following manner. In deficit countries (which are experiencing a loss of money balances), the government reduces the quantity of fiduciary money in circulation so that the total quantity of money decreases more than it would as a consequence of financing the BOP deficit. In surplus countries (those experiencing monetary inflows), the central bank increases the quantity of

Exhibit 4.2

Central bank sterilization of international money flows

A.	Deficit country	
	Change in money supply resulting from BOP deficit	−
	Fiduciary money issue by the Central bank	+
	Net change in the money supply	0
B.	Surplus country	
	Change in money supply resulting from BOP surplus	+
	Fiduciary money issue by the Central bank	−
	Net change in the money supply	0

fiduciary money. Now, the increase in the money supply is greater than it would be as a consequence of the BOP surplus. If governments behave in this fashion, adjustment toward a BOP equilibrium occurs more rapidly than it would in the case of pure commodity money.

A more likely scenario is where government monetary policy retards the Hume adjustment mechanism. This case is more probable because governments, especially in those countries experiencing BOP deficits, are often tempted to offset money supply changes resulting from BOP disequilibria. When this happens, government sterilizes money flows. Automatic restoration of BOP equilibrium now occurs more slowly, and not at all in cases of perfect sterilization.

Exhibit 4.2 summarizes the monetary changes occurring when central banks perfectly sterilize monetary flows. In each country, government fiduciary money creation (or destruction) perfectly offsets money flows initiated by a BOP disequilibrium. Because, the money supply in both countries does not change, neither does the price level. Relative prices in the two countries remain unchanged, and government monetary policies have effectively neutralized the mechanism of Hume. BOP disequilibria are not automatically eliminated, and deficits or surpluses persist.

There are limits to government sterilization of money flows. If a deficit country continues to increase the quantity of fiduciary money to offset the loss of specie to other countries, the ratio of commodity money (monetary gold, G_M) to fiduciary money (FG_M) in the country declines. Long before this ratio reaches its lower limit of zero, the ability of financial institutions to convert fiduciary money into commodity money is jeopardized. That occurs when depositors sense that they might not be able to convert their fiduciary money into commodity money on demand. Desirous of avoiding a financial panic, governments cease issuing additional fiduciary money and sterilization ceases. Hence, in the long run, Hume's mechanism remains valid.[3]

CHAPTER 5

Foreign Exchange Markets With Fiat Money: Fixed Exchange Rates

Arguments for Leaving the Gold Standard

While major trading countries abandoned fiduciary money when they went off the gold standard in the 1930s, they did not abandon fixed exchange rates. Imposition of fiat money was accompanied by government price-fixing in foreign exchange markets. Prior to examining these arrangements, two popular arguments for leaving the gold standard are examined.

Domestic Monetary Autonomy

One was that leaving the gold standard would give individual countries more latitude for conducting an independent monetary policy. The ideas of British economist J. M. Keynes were gaining popularity at the time. It was his contention that governments should play a more active role in attempting to stabilize their national economies.

Fiduciary money arrangements obstruct such policy activism. That is because the quantity of money in an individual country partly is a result of changes in the global economy and, thus, not strictly under the control of the national monetary authority. For an individual country, changes in its money supply can occur as a result of changes in the domestic production of commodity money, the issue of fiduciary money, or both. However, they are also affected by the balance of payments (BOP) position of the country. Countries with BOP deficits are net exporters of money; those with a surplus, net importers.

With such monetary interdependence, individual countries are exposed to monetary shocks originating elsewhere. Assume, for example, the discovery of a rich new vein of gold in South Africa. Under a fiduciary money arrangement such as the gold standard, the increased supply of money results in higher prices in South Africa. With fixed exchange rates, South African goods become less competitive in international markets, and that country experiences a BOP deficit. Money flows out of the country, and inflation originating in South Africa is transmitted to the rest of the world via fixed exchange rates. These adjustments continue until monetary equilibrium is reestablished. Note that while the original monetary disturbance occurs in a single country, resolution of the disturbance is a global matter.

While fiduciary money systems are characterized by monetary interdependence, it does not follow that replacing them with fiat money necessarily will bring greater national monetary autonomy. Many countries adopting fiat money with fixed exchange rates discovered this. They found they simply had substituted one type of convertibility problem for another.

One convertibility problem is eliminated when issuers of paper money no longer are obliged to convert that money into commodity money on demand. Individual countries, however, are not free to select the monetary policy of their choice unless, of course, that choice just happens to be consistent with the monetary policies of other countries. If it is not consistent, the country often confronts a second type of convertibility problem.

To illustrate, assume that a country chooses to issue fiat money at a much more rapid rate than do other countries. It experiences a BOP deficit. The money that is shipped overseas to finance the BOP deficit returns to the country, and depletes its foreign exchange reserves (held by the central bank). With no foreign exchange reserves, the central bank no longer can repatriate foreign-owned money which it originally issued. The country now faces the second kind of convertibility problem. Central bank refusal to repatriate its own currency means that the currency of the country becomes a nonconvertible currency in the international economy. That is, traders in other countries will no longer accept this currency in payment for goods and services.[1] To avoid this plight, the country must sacrifice monetary autonomy and adopt a less expansionary monetary policy. Thus, when a country adopts a fiat money standard with fixed exchange rates, a high degree of monetary interdependence still exists.

Parenthetically, not all economists consider such monetary interdependence undesirable. It is manifested in the form of market discipline, something those in the Austrian tradition most often view favorably.[2] According to them, we are much better off in a world where monetary authorities have less discretion to conduct policy. They cite the nearly eight decades of continuous fiat money inflation as testimony to what happens when monetary authorities are given too much discretion. In their judgment, only the restoration of fiduciary money will provide the discipline necessary for monetary authorities to limit money growth.

Economic Instability

A second argument against the use of fiduciary money is that it results in excessive economic instability. This argument is based upon the adjustment process delineated by Hume. Countries experiencing a BOP deficit finance those deficits by exporting money. Surplus countries, on the other hand, are net importers of money balances. The resulting redistribution of the world's money supply occasions adjustments in prices and nominal incomes in both deficit and surplus countries. According to critics of fiduciary money, this adjustment process generates continuous economic fluctuations which are inherent under a fiduciary money standard.

The relevant consideration, however, is not whether economic instability occurs with fiduciary money. It does. The question is whether a fiduciary money standard (such as the gold standard) is more prone to economic instability than are alternative standards. The appropriate comparison here is with the fiat money.

The question is much more complex when formulated this way, and not easily resolved from an analytical perspective. Clearly two types of instability are involved—price and income instability. The more difficult one is income instability, or variation in real output as measured in physical units. It is considered first.

With fiduciary money (and without perfect sterilization of gold flows), BOP disequilibria do cause nominal income to vary. Whether changes in nominal income result in variations in real output is critical. If they do not, the potential impact of BOP disequilibria on aggregate production and the employment of resources is very limited.

Alternatively, if changes in nominal income do have a significant impact on the level of production and the employment of resources, then BOP disequilibria are contributing to business cycle fluctuations. Because the argument here is that changes in the money supply are responsible for fluctuations in economic activity, it is an argument shared by economists with a monetary theory of the business cycle. Among those economists are Irving Fisher, R. G. Hawtrey, and, more recently, Milton Friedman.

The difficulty here is that business cycles are complex phenomena, and there is no consensus among economists concerning root causes. Only a minority of economists proffer monetary explanations. From an analytical standpoint, the majority of economists not citing monetary causes are less likely to fret about BOP disequilibria and their potential for generating economic instability under the fiduciary money standard.

In cases where monetary disturbances with fiduciary money do lead to variations in real output and employment, there is no assurance that these variations are greater than would occur with fiat money. Empirical data indicate otherwise. Variations in the money supply have been much greater since the adoption of fiat money than they were with fiduciary money. Because the perceived problem with a fiduciary money standard revolves around the instability of money, these data suggest a much greater likelihood of income instability with fiat money.

A second type of instability is price instability. The argument that there is greater price instability under a fiduciary money standard is a very weak one. It is supported by neither data nor theory. Economic analysis suggests that we are likely to experience greater long-run price stability if we use commodity or fiduciary money rather than fiat money. The reason is that, with commodity or fiduciary money, there are market forces in operation that tend to bring about long-run price stability. That analysis was developed in Chapter 2.

There are no such automatic market forces to check movements in the general price level under a fiat money standard. Elimination of the convertibility option (under fiduciary money) and the imposition of fiat money gave central banks of individual countries much greater monetary autonomy. They have exercised this new freedom to greatly expand the quantity of money. The result has been secular worldwide inflation. The cumulative effect is the destruction of the purchasing power of most fiat monies throughout the world. For a comparison of the relative stability of the value of money under fiduciary and fiat money standards, refer to the U.S. experience portrayed in Figure 2.1 in Chapter 2.

Government Price-Fixing in Economically Advanced Countries: The Adjustable Peg System

Fixed exchange rates with fiat money occur when exchange rates are set by government. These fixed exchange rates do not reflect the relative commodity content of different monies, nor are they the result of market trading activity. They come directly from the minds of politicians or government bureaucrats. These prices frequently are referred to as official exchange rates, possibly in an effort to give them legitimacy.

Government price-fixing arrangements were quite popular in the 20th century, especially in countries with a penchant for economic planning and government regulation of the economy. Examples are found in both economically advanced countries and in less developed countries. In this section, a historical episode of government price-fixing by economically advanced countries is examined. The arrangement was utilized for pricing foreign exchange during much of the middle third of the 20th century.

The adjustable peg system, as the price-fixing arrangement was called, emerged from a meeting in Bretton Woods, New Hampshire, USA, in 1944. At the time, it was apparent that World War II would end in victory by the allied countries. Economists and finance ministers of these countries were meeting to discuss institutional arrangements which would encourage an expansion of world trade in the post–World War II period. Their deliberations resulted in the formation of the International Monetary Fund (IMF) as an organization and the adjustable-peg system as a mechanism for government pricing of foreign exchange.

Major Objectives of the IMF

Founders of the IMF wished to accomplish three major objectives: (1) elimination of exchange controls, (2) national autonomy in the conduct of monetary policy, and (3) reasonable stability of exchange rates.

Exchange controls are government imposed regulations for allocating foreign exchange. Anyone buying and selling foreign exchange must have prior governmental approval. A practical consequence is that individuals wishing to make purchases from abroad not only must have the willingness to do so, but permission from the government as well. By making it more difficult to acquire foreign exchange, exchange controls impede the flow of international trade. Removing those controls has the opposite effect. World trade increases and economic agents capture gains from trade they were unable to with exchange controls. World living standards improve.

In addition to eliminating exchange controls, the IMF also supported efforts by major trading countries to move to an entirely new type of monetary standard. One by one, countries left the old gold standard in favor of new fiat money. A principal motive was to replace the international money of the 19th century with national currencies. Domestic monetary autonomy was deemed more important than adherence to an international monetary standard. This perspective was consistent with the policy proposals of British economist John M. Keynes, who argued that an independent national monetary policy was necessary if national governments were to have the requisite freedom to pursue policies that would make their economies more stable.

New national currencies were to be traded for one another in foreign exchange markets characterized by stable exchange rates. The desire for reasonable stability of exchange rates largely was a response to the international monetary climate that prevailed during the 1930s. Many countries were mired in the Great Depression and were experiencing relatively low levels of production and employment. In an effort to extricate themselves from this situation, countries often devalued their currencies with the objective of increasing domestic production and employment at the expense of employment abroad.

Policies that attempted to export unemployment in this manner were referred to as "beggar thy neighbor" policies. There was a fundamental problem with this particular strategy, however. Devaluation by one country frequently was met by offsetting devaluations by the affected countries. Exchange rates became more volatile. The results were often perverse— sacrifices of the gains from trade and decreases in total volumes of world production and trade, but little or no gain in domestic employment.

Replacing this with a system of stable exchange rates was viewed as crucial by the architects of the IMF. Nevertheless, they were aware that some flexibility in exchange rates would, at times, be necessary. The result, by design, was the adjustable-peg system. It combined elements of both fixed and flexible rates. Exchange rates were fixed, but with a mechanism for adjusting them if they were inappropriate. This was the mechanism for delivering reasonable stability of exchange rates.

The fixed exchange rates were established by government price-fixing in the market for a commodity with a rich monetary history—gold. Each country fixed the price of gold in terms of its money. Setting the price of gold in this manner resulted in a fixed exchange rate for each pair of currencies. For example, if the United Kingdom prices gold at $14£$ per ounce, and the United States prices gold at $35 per ounce, then a fixed exchange rate exists between the dollar and the pound: $1£ = \$2.50$.[3]

As is always the case, the following question arises when government sets the price in a market: What happens if this fixed price is not a market clearing one? That is the case in Figure 5.1, where the United Kingdom is running a BOP deficit with the United States. At the exchange rate of $\$2.5 = 1£$, there is an excess supply of pounds in the market $(S_1 - D_1)$.

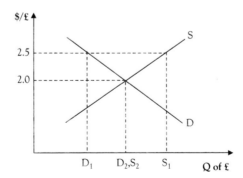

Figure 5.1 *Market for British pounds*

Notes: £ = British pound, D = demand, S = supply

The Hume mechanism will not assure us of market clearing because each country is conducting an independent monetary policy. That is, monetary authorities may choose to offset the effects of money shipments to settle disequilibria in the BOP. If that is the case in this instance, the central bank in the United Kingdom (the Bank of England) must be prepared to redeem the excess pounds British citizens are shipping overseas. In doing so, they draw upon the foreign exchange holdings of the Bank of England.

The international reserves of any central bank are finite. A problem arises when the holdings of the Bank of England approach zero in the limit. The IMF made provision for such a contingency. If the BOP problem was perceived as *temporary*, the United Kingdom was permitted to borrow reserves from the IMF.[4] The Bank of England could, in this case, use the borrowed reserves to redeem any excess pounds flowing back to the bank as a consequence of the country's BOP deficit.

In situations where the BOP problem is considered *fundamental* (i.e., secular), a country was permitted (after consultation with the IMF) to adjust the peg. This involved changing the official price of gold. Governments in deficit countries would devalue their currencies, or increase the price of gold. In the present example, the UK government increases the price of gold to 17.5£ per ounce. This constitutes a 25 percent devaluation of the British pound (3.5£/14£ = 0.25).

The new fixed exchange rate between the dollar and the pound is now $2 = 1£. Since the value of the pound has fallen, people in the United States find British goods and services less expensive than before. Additional purchases cause them to buy more pounds in the foreign exchange market. The quantity demanded of pounds increases. In addition, since it now requires 0.5£ to purchase a U.S. dollar instead of 0.4£, all U.S. goods and services become more expensive for British citizens. When they respond by purchasing less, the quantity of pounds supplied in the foreign exchange market decreases. In Figure 5.1, the new foreign exchange rate clears the market, that is, the UK balance of payments now is in balance.

Problems With the Adjustable Peg

This mechanism for pricing foreign exchange was operational for nearly three decades (1944 to 1971). During that period, countries reduced barriers to international trade.[5] The volume of world trade responded by expanding significantly. Not only did postwar economies not return to the depressed economic conditions of the 1930s (as many followers of Keynes had predicted), but many countries also experienced secular improvements in living standards.

Despite the longevity of the adjustable-peg system, there were three serious structural flaws within the system that led to its ultimate demise: (1) the operational objectives of the system were inconsistent; (2) the adjustable peg was not very adjustable in practice; and (3) the system encouraged massive speculation against weak currencies.

Inconsistent Objectives

While the adjustable-peg system was designed as a blend of fixed and flexible exchange rates, in practice, it was essentially a system of fixed rates. The major difficulty with the arrangement was that the objectives of the system were inconsistent. Fixed exchange rates (objective 3) were not consistent with national autonomy in the conduct of monetary policy (objective 2). Indeed, those attempting to simultaneously accomplish objectives (2) and (3) were faced with the following dilemma. Fixed exchange rates work best when all countries follow more or less the same monetary policies. However, if all countries must follow roughly the same monetary policy, there is no national monetary autonomy.

The following example illustrates the point. Assume that two countries, the United States and Mexico, produce an identical product— shoes. The exchange rate between the Mexican peso and the U.S. dollar is fixed at 10 pesos = $1 (or 1 peso = $0.10). Moreover, assume that the initial price (in Year 0) for the shoes is the same in the two countries even though they are priced in different currencies. As shown in Exhibit 5.1, one can purchase the shoes in Mexico for 500 pesos or in the United States for $50. At these prices, consumers are indifferent between purchasing the shoes in Mexico or the United States.

The BOP between the two countries also is initially in balance (Figure 5.2, point A). Now, assume that the United States and Mexico follow dramatically different monetary policies. The U.S. central bank, sensitive to the potential for inflation, holds its money supply constant, that is, the annual growth rate for money is 0 percent. By contrast, Mexico's

Exhibit 5.1

Money and price growth in Mexico and the United States

	Annual growth			Price of shoes	
Country	M	P		Year 0	Year 1
United States	0	0		$50	$50
Mexico	100	100		500p	1,000p

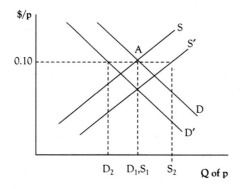

Figure 5.2 Market for Mexican pesos

Notes: p = pesos, D = demand, S = supply

monetary authorities choose to increase the money supply at a rate of 100 percent per year.

Assuming that price changes exactly mirror money growth rates, the price level doubles in Mexico. In the United States, it remains the same. If shoe prices move in tandem with the general price level, the price of shoes in Mexico in Year 1 is now 1,000 pesos. They remain at $50 in the United States. Given a fixed exchange rate, it now will be cheaper for consumers in both countries to purchase shoes in the United States. For Americans to purchase the shoes in Mexico, the price now is $100 (vs. $50 in the United States) because that sum is required to purchase 1,000 pesos in the foreign exchange market. For Mexicans, the cost of purchasing shoes in the United States is 500 pesos (vs. 1,000 pesos in Mexico), or the cost of buying $50 in the foreign exchange market.

As a consequence of the markedly different monetary policies, producers of shoes in Mexico no longer are competitive with their U.S. counterparts. Moreover, the problem is much more general than that of selling shoes. The prices of nearly all Mexican products will have increased sharply in comparison to prices in the United States and consumers will prefer the relatively less expensive U.S. products in these markets as well. The result is a deterioration in the BOP for Mexico.

In Figure 5.2, the supply curve for Mexican pesos shifts to the right because more Mexicans now wish to exchange pesos for U.S. dollars to buy U.S. products. Likewise, the demand curve for pesos shifts to the left as fewer Americans than before are interested in importing Mexican products. Rather than a payments balance, Mexico now has a BOP deficit in the amount of $(0.10) (S_2 - D_2)$.

This BOP problem experienced by Mexico is the direct result of the inconsistencies of objectives (2) and (3). Fixed exchange rates are not consistent with an autonomous monetary policy in Mexico. Government officials now have a policy dilemma. They can restrict capital flows (the outflow of money) through restrictive trade policies such as exchange controls, quotas, or higher tariffs. However, this action reduces living standards by limiting the gains from trade. Alternatively, the Bank of Mexico can sacrifice its monetary autonomy by reducing its money growth rate so that it is in conformity with that of the United States.

Adjustable-Peg Not Very Adjustable

A second difficulty with the pricing mechanism of the IMF was that, in practice, the adjustable peg was not very adjustable. Indeed, use of the term adjustable peg was a misnomer. Only rarely was the peg adjusted, and that was after a BOP problem had reached crisis proportions.

There were two reasons for this. First, the successful implementation of the system required behavior on the part of bureaucrats that was beyond their capacity to deliver. For each BOP problem, they were to determine whether it was temporary or fundamental. For this distinction to be meaningful, designation of a problem as fundamental must occur prior to its deterioration into a crisis situation.

This may sound simple in concept, but it is not easily accomplished. Any BOP position results from payments flows generated by multitudes of transactions undertaken by thousands of individuals. These individuals have differing motivations and frequently are responding to different stimuli. Forecasting their aggregate behavior is very difficult, if not impossible. Thus, it is not surprising that bureaucrats responsible for implementing the adjustable peg system had difficulty distinguishing between temporary and fundamental disequilibria. Given a reluctance to classify problems as fundamental, the arrangement most often worked out to be one of fixed exchange rates.

Second, the adjustable peg system was designed as if it were to be carried out in a political vacuum. Nothing could be further from the truth. Those responsible for administering the system were bureaucrats and politicians. For them, the decision of whether to adjust the peg was not strictly based on economic logic, but upon political considerations as well. Prior to adjusting the peg, they must be convinced that the political benefits of such action outweigh the costs. Furthermore, this criterion must be met even when it is clear that the BOP problem is a fundamental one.

Consequently, political factors also militated against adjusting exchange rates. To more fully understand why that is the case, it is helpful to recognize that government price-fixing in foreign exchange markets is just a special case of government price-fixing more generally. Once a government makes the decision to regulate prices, it often finds it difficult to change them.

Price inertia occurs because the pricing process has become politicized. Whenever a price changes, some individuals find themselves better off while others are worse off. If the price change occurs as a consequence of market forces, individuals who are harmed are more prone to view the situation as one where they undertook risks and the outcome was unfavorable. This is decidedly not the case once price determination is politicized. Those who are harmed by a price change know exactly why they are worse off. They are worse off because a government official decided to change the price.

Understandably, their response is political. Sometimes those harmed petition the government. Sometimes they riot in the streets. On occasion, the reaction is strong enough that governments are removed from power, either through the ballot box or in a less democratic manner. Aware of these possibilities, governments often become conservative and refuse to change the price even when economic fundamentals would dictate such action.

The situation in the United Kingdom during the 1960s provides an excellent example of regulatory price inertia under the adjustable peg system. After a series of BOP deficits, it became clear that the pound was overvalued relative to the market assessment. In the terminology of the IMF, the United Kingdom had a fundamental BOP problem. Nevertheless, the UK government was reluctant to adjust the peg. That reticence largely was politically based. The United Kingdom imported much of its food, and any devaluation of significance would sharply increase food prices. If the government were to devalue, critics (such as opposing political parties) would quickly point out that the burden of adjustment falls disproportionately upon the working classes and poor people in the country. Aware of this potential criticism, the government refused to devalue until the problem had reached crisis proportions.

In addition to the fact that exchange rate changes rearrange balance sheets, emotional elements also entered the picture. A stable exchange rate over extended periods of time was a matter of national pride. Many governments maintained that their currency was as good as gold. The U.S. government made pronouncements of this nature in the 1950s and 1960s. It did so to assure foreign holders of dollar balances that they need not be concerned about the quality of their holdings even though the United States was running continuous BOP deficits. Those who believed such assertions found their net worth reduced when the U.S. government devalued the dollar in 1971.

Adjustable Peg Encouraged Speculation

A third difficulty was that the adjustable peg system encouraged speculation against weak currencies, or currencies of countries with continuous BOP deficits and limited foreign exchange reserves. As a speculator, how would you like an institutional arrangement that permitted you to speculate in markets where there were two possible outcomes: (1) you win and (2) you break even? This is what the adjustable peg system offered. All that was required of speculators was that they identify currencies for which there was a reasonably good chance of devaluation. This identification was not difficult. Virtually everyone had knowledge of countries with serious BOP problems, and whose currencies were under pressure in foreign exchange markets.

Consider again the case of the British pound with an official value of $2.50 (Figure 5.3). At that price, there is excess supply of pounds (S_1 – D_1). Assume that the pound is a weak currency in the sense described earlier. The United Kingdom has borrowed heavily from the IMF, but to no avail. At the current exchange rate, borrowed reserves are quickly shipped overseas to finance the continuing BOP deficit. Pressure on the pound is heavy, and speculators perceive that the Bank of England is likely to devalue.

Having identified this candidate for devaluation, what do speculators do? They sell the asset they expect to decline in value (pounds) and buy the asset they expect to increase in value (dollars). Assume that a speculator sells 100,000£ in exchange for $250,000. What are the possible outcomes? One is that the Bank of England does devalue, and that the price of the dollar moves from 0.4£ to 0.5£ (the price of the pound drops from $2.50 to $2.00). Our speculator now exchanges his or her $250,000 for 125,000£, a profit of 25,000£. If, on the other hand, the Bank of England does not devalue, the speculator converts the $250,000 back into 100,000£. He or she breaks even. There is no chance that the Bank of England will revalue the pound (decrease the official price of gold), which would cause our speculator to experience a loss.

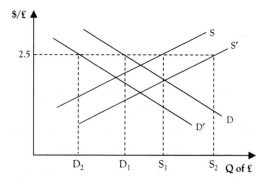

Figure 5.3 Market for British pounds

Notes: £ = British pound, D = demand, S = supply

Such speculative activity does make the BOP problem worse. Those demanding dollars in this market are supplying pounds. As speculators reduce pound holdings in favor of dollars, the supply curve in Figure 5.3 shifts to the right (from S to S'). Those demanding pounds in this market are supplying dollars. In anticipation of a possible devaluation, many of these individuals delay or cancel plans to acquire pounds. As a consequence, the demand curve for pounds shifts to the left (from D to D'). The UK balance of payments deficit now is $2.5 \times (S_2 - D_2)$ instead of $2.5 \times (S_1 - D_1)$, that is, the deficit is larger on account of speculative activity.

While speculative activity can aggravate a BOP problem, it does not follow that speculators caused the problem. This deserves mention because governments frequently are unwilling to admit their role in a BOP problem. Rather, they seek to place the blame elsewhere. Speculators are a convenient target. Thus, it is not uncommon to hear central bankers (or politicians) say: Our nation is currently experiencing a severe BOP shortfall, and the underlying problem is one of excessive speculation.

To the contrary, speculators most likely play a stabilizing role in such situations. In our current example, at a price of $2.50, the British pound is overvalued relative to the price consistent with the plans of private traders. It is this price distortion which is responsible for any chaotic conditions that exist in the market. By increasing the cost of resisting devaluation, speculative activity hastens the adjustment of the exchange rate in the direction of a market clearing one.

Foreign Exchange Markets With Fiat Money: Government Price-Fixing in Less Developed Countries

Although most major trading countries have abandoned fixed exchange rates, some less developed countries have not. Fixed exchange rates in these countries are not the result of actions by private traders. Rather, they represent decisions made by government bureaucrats and politicians. In this respect, fixed exchange rates in less developed countries are no different from price-fixing arrangements in more highly developed countries.

One must invariably ask the following question when confronted by a fixed price in a market. What happens if the fixed price is not a market clearing one? This usually is not a significant problem when governments initially regulate prices because they often select the current market price as the regulated price. In Figure 5.4a, for example, the government of Tanzania fixes the price of the U.S. dollar at 100 Tanzanian shillings (TSH). Because this is the market-clearing price, there is no BOP problem. The quantity of dollars supplied at this price is equal to the quantity demanded. The outcome is the same as it would be if the price were market determined.

There is little likelihood, however, that both the government-determined price and the market price will remain equal. Differences in monetary policies, for one thing, militate against it. In a world of fiat money, individual governments are free to determine the quantity of money in their country. This will not create a serious problem if money growth in Tanzania is similar to money growth in the United States. That is not the case here. Tanzania increases the quantity of fiat money at a much faster rate than does the United States. These disparities in money growth rates are reflected in differences in the growth rates of prices.

The result is not surprising. As illustrated in Figure 5.4b, the fixed price of 100 TSH = $1 no longer is a market clearing one. Because prices in Tanzania increased more rapidly than they did in the United States, Tanzanian goods have lost price-competitiveness. As a consequence, the demand curve for dollars shifts to the right (from D to D′) and the supply curve shifts to the left (from S to S′). The Tanzanian shilling now is overvalued relative to how the market would price the currency. The result is an excess demand for dollars in the market ($D_2 - S_2$), that is, Tanzania is experiencing BOP difficulties.

There are consequences if a country such as Tanzania maintains an inflationary monetary policy but resists devaluation. First, the central bank draws down its holdings of foreign exchange reserves to finance its BOP deficits. In the limit, these reserves approach zero. Second, the ability of a country to borrow additional reserves from international lending agencies (such as the IMF) diminishes. Once such agencies become concerned about the country's ability to repay its debts, they may refuse to lend additional reserves. With a continuing shortage of foreign exchange, the central bank has but two choices. It can acquiesce to market forces and adjust the exchange rate for TSH downward. Alternatively, it can attempt to circumvent the market by restricting capital (or money) flows.

(a)

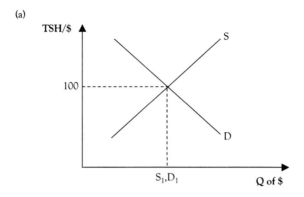

(b)

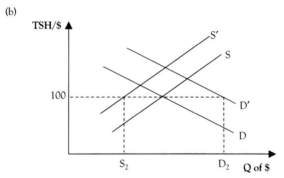

(c)

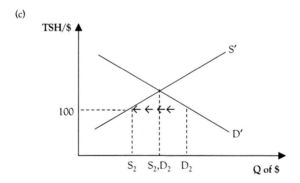

Figure 5.4 Market for U.S. dollars

Notes: TSH = Tanzanian shillings, D = demand, S = supply

How governments in this situation respond depends on whether they are committed to preserving (or increasing) trade flows. When the major trading countries fixed foreign exchange prices under the adjustable peg system, they usually gave high priority to accommodating demand for foreign exchange and increasing world trade. Many governments in less developed countries have not. When confronted with the choice of adjusting exchange rates or restricting capital flows, many have opted for managed trade. In foreign exchange markets, managed trade means that central banks limit access to foreign exchange rather than accommodate the demand for foreign exchange.

In Figure 5.4c, the Bank of Tanzania attempts to suppress the level of demand for foreign exchange along the path indicated by the arrows. The objective is to force quantity demanded to the level of available supply (S_2). If successful, trade flows are reduced because the quantity of foreign exchange traded (S_2) is below levels traded when central banks accommodate demand (D_2) or when they devalue to the equilibrium price ($S_3 = D_3$).

Consequences of an Overvalued Exchange Rate

Decisions by governments in less developed countries to fix the price of foreign exchange and to maintain an overvalued exchange rate (relative to market valuation) influences the structure of foreign exchange markets. Such policies invariably lead to the implementation of exchange controls. In addition, they limit the medium of exchange function of money if the currencies of these countries become nonconvertible. Finally, their policies often encourage black markets in foreign exchange.

Exchange Controls

Exchange controls are government laws that attempt to strictly regulate the form of foreign exchange transactions. Although there is some variation from country to country, they generally take the following form. All economic agents (domestic and foreign) engaging in foreign exchange transactions are restricted to making exchanges with the government. Those selling foreign exchange must sell to the government. Likewise, buyers are only permitted to purchase from the government. Normally, government participation is through the central bank or an agent of the bank (e.g., a designated commercial bank).

The function of exchange controls is to allocate foreign exchange when price is not permitted to assume this role. In Figure 5.4c, for example, the dollar is undervalued relative to how the market would price it. At the government-determined price, there is excess demand for dollars. With exchange controls, economic agents must not only have the willingness to purchase foreign exchange but governmental approval as well. Government intent is to suppress effective demand (along the path of arrows) to the level of the available supply. This is accomplished by denying requests for foreign exchange in the amount of $D_2 - S_2$.

When administratively allocating foreign exchange, governments typically apply the following guidelines. Foreign exchange will be allocated to those who propose to use it for essential purposes, but will be denied to those who propose to use it for other (nonessential) purposes. An essential purpose generally is one that is consistent with broad policy goals decreed by the government. Examples of such goals are economic growth, capital formation, and increased agricultural output. Nonessential purposes are those that are not consistent with such policy goals. Requests for foreign exchange to purchase consumer luxury goods are an example.

Government pricing and allocation of foreign exchange politicizes the market, and equity issues soon arise. Individuals may fail to acquire foreign exchange, not because they are unwilling to pay the price, but because some government official decided that they would not receive the foreign exchange. Moreover, those administering the allocation process often have a broader interpretation of who qualifies as an essential user of foreign exchange. It can include (among others) brothers-in-law, other family members, members of the same tribe, or old secondary school cronies. Such behavior further aggravates equity concerns about the allocation of foreign exchange.

In addition to politicizing foreign exchange markets, exchange controls impose heavy costs on a country's citizens. A major cost is a significant reduction in economic freedom. Exchange controls restrict whom individuals trade with, the number and quality of goods and services available for them to purchase, and where they are allowed to travel. Travel restrictions occur because foreign travel normally is classified as a nonessential use of foreign exchange. Especially, heavy bearers of these costs are the relatively poor, who often lack the necessary political connections to gain access to foreign exchange.

Exchange controls also lower living standards. They reduce the gains from trade that result from voluntary exchange. Individuals must substitute less preferred for more preferred choices. For some, it might mean purchasing an additional item of clothing instead of the more preferred visit to relatives in a neighboring country. Others may have to forego employment opportunities that are no longer possible. In each of these cases, the result is the same: a reduction in economic welfare.

Nonconvertible Currencies

A convertible currency is one that can be converted readily into another currency of one's choice. For this reason, convertible currencies are accepted by market participants as international exchange media. Nearly all international trade is conducted with these monies, with the U.S. dollar the most popular. Nonconvertible currencies, by contrast, cannot be converted readily into another currency of one's choice. Consequently, they generally are not accepted as payment in international transactions.

To better understand the distinction between convertible and nonconvertible currencies, consider the series of transactions which are summarized in Exhibits 5.2 and 5.3. Each transaction is numbered. They involve an overseas purchase and the tracing of the monetary claim used to finance the purchase.

Individual A in country A purchases goods (G) from Firm B in country B. Payment is made by a check (Chk_A) drawn on Bank A, which also is in country A. The transaction is recorded as (1) in the balance sheet of both participants (Exhibit 5.2). Individual A shows an increase in its inventory of goods on the asset side of its balance sheet. The check used to make the purchase (Chk_A) is the offsetting liability. Firm B swaps assets. It now owns a check (denominated in foreign money) which it acquired by drawing down its inventory of goods.

Firm B is interested in domestic money—not the foreign money it received in exchange. Thus, it sends the check to its commercial bank (Bank B1), and receives demand deposits (denominated in domestic

Exhibit 5.2
T-accounts for an international transaction

Individual A			Firm B	
1) Goods +	1) Chk$_A$ +		1) Goods −	
6) DD −	6) Chk$_A$ −		1) Chk$_A$ +	
			2) Chk$_A$ −	
			2) DD +	

Bank A			Bank B1	
5) Chk$_A$ +			2) Chk$_A$ +	2) DD +
5) MBD −			3) Chk$_A$ −	
6) Chk$_A$ −	6) DD −		3) MBD +	

Central Bank A			Central Bank B	
4) Chk$_A$ +	4) Chk$_{B2}$ +		3) Chk$_A$ +	3) MBD +
5) Chk$_A$ −	5) MBD −		4) Chk$_A$ −	
8) DD$_F$ −	8) Chk$_{B2}$ −		4) Chk$_{B2}$ +	
			7) Chk$_{B2}$ −	7) MBD −

Bank B2	
7) Chk$_{B2}$ +	
7) MBD −	
8) Chk$_{B2}$ −	8) DD$_F$ −

money) in exchange. This transaction is recorded in the balance sheet of both participants as (2). Bank B1 holds the check, which it acquired by increasing the deposit balance of Firm B. Bank B1 now sends the check to the central bank and receives deposit credit for it, that is, its deposit balance (MBD) at the central bank increased in the amount of the check. Central Bank B now owns the foreign monetary claim (Chk$_A$). The deposit balance of Bank B1 is the offsetting entry. These transactions are recorded as (3) in the balance sheets of the participants.

Because the check is a foreign monetary claim, the central bank in country B has several options. It could deposit the check in a bank in country A, and increase its holdings of foreign exchange reserves. Instead, Central Bank B presents the monetary claim to the central bank in country A (Central Bank A). It requests a monetary claim denominated in its own money, and receives a check drawn by Central Bank A on Bank B2 in country B. Note that this decision by Central Bank B will have the effect of reducing the foreign exchange reserves of Central Bank A. This transaction involving the two central banks is recorded as (4). Each bank gives up a check denominated in the currency of the other country in exchange for one denominated in its own currency.

Both central banks proceed to clear the checks. In country A, Central Bank A sends the check it received to the bank upon which it is drawn (Bank A). Because it is giving up an instrument of value, it reduces the deposit balance of Bank A at the central bank by the same amount. Bank A now holds Chk_A that it obtained by reducing its cash balance at Central Bank A. The entries associated with this transaction are entered as (5). In transaction (6), Bank A cancels the check, and reduces the deposit balance of Individual A. The check originally issued to finance the imported goods now has cleared the banking system.

In country B, Central Bank B sends Chk_{B2} to the bank upon which it is drawn (Bank B2), and reduces the balance of that bank at the central bank (MBD) by the same amount—transaction (7). As the final transaction (8), Bank B2 cancels the check and reduces the deposit balance (DD_F) of the drawer. The drawer, in this case, is Central Bank A. Because this deposit balance was a portion of Central Bank A's foreign exchange holdings, country A's foreign exchange reserves are now lower. The origin of this loss of reserves was the importation of goods by Individual A. For a summary of net balance sheet changes for all participants, refer to Exhibit 5.3.

In this example, the currency of country A is a convertible currency. The critical transaction in this sequence is (4). With that exchange of checks, Central Bank A repatriated a monetary instrument from Country A that had been sent overseas to finance a purchase. So long as Central Bank A continues this practice, the country will have a convertible currency. Overseas traders accepting Country A's money will have no difficulty exchanging it for their currency of choice.

Exhibit 5.3
Net changes in balance sheets

Country A		Country B	
Private nonbank sector		**Private nonbank sector**	
Goods +		Goods –	
DD –		DD +	

Bank sector		Bank sector	
MBD –	DD –		DD +
			DD_F –

Central bank A		Central bank B	
DD_F –	MBD –		

If, on the other hand, Central Bank A refuses Central Bank B's request to exchange monies, Central Bank B is left holding a foreign monetary instrument (from country A) that it is unable to convert into its own money. Once this happens, Central Bank B will no longer accept bank drafts drawn upon banks in country A. Commercial banks and other economic agents in country B (and other countries), likewise, will refuse such drafts. At this point, country A's money ceases to be an international medium of exchange. In other words, it is a nonconvertible currency.

The government of a country determines whether its currency is convertible or nonconvertible. Countries with nonconvertible currencies have them because their governments chose to have nonconvertible currencies. This decision most often is not made directly, but is a by-product of other decisions. The first is the decision by a government to fix the price of its currency in foreign exchange markets. This, by itself, is not sufficient for a country to have a nonconvertible currency. What normally is required, as well, is a monetary policy that results in inflation rates appreciably higher than those of competitors. Countries with conservative monetary policies can blend government price-fixing in foreign exchange markets with convertible currencies. The major trading countries did so under the (IMF's) adjustable-peg system.

Many less developed countries, however, have combined rapid monetary growth with fixed exchange rates established by the government. The consequences are quite predictable. These countries usually run BOP deficits. By accommodating the excess demand for foreign exchange, they exhaust their holdings of foreign exchange reserves. When these reserves approach zero in the limit, a country has three choices. First, it can choose to let the market determine the price of its currency. Second, it can adopt a more restrictive monetary policy. Or, third, it can move to a nonconvertible currency. Countries with nonconvertible currencies have selected the last option.

The decision by a government to have a nonconvertible currency has important monetary implications for its citizens. They now face a dual monetary economy. While it is possible for them to use money issued by their government to make domestic purchases, they cannot use that money when making foreign purchases. The latter require payment in convertible currencies that other countries issue.[8]

A more important monetary implication of the use of nonconvertible currencies is that they reinforce the effectiveness of exchange controls. If a country has exchange controls but a convertible currency, economic agents can attempt to circumvent controls by using domestic money to pay for foreign goods. With a nonconvertible currency, however, that option is not available. One must pay with foreign money, and compliance with foreign exchange control laws means obtaining that money from the government. Obtaining foreign money, however, may not be possible where governments routinely deny access to foreign exchange.

Black Markets

Government price-fixing in foreign exchange markets is a necessary condition for the existence of black markets. Remove the price-fixing and there is no black market. The reason is simple. If traders are free to establish the price, they will do so at a level that will clear the market. In Figure 5.5, this occurs at the price of 300 TSH per dollar. At this price, all those willing to buy and sell are able to do so. Thus, there is no economic incentive to devote resources to the activity of reallocating available foreign exchange.

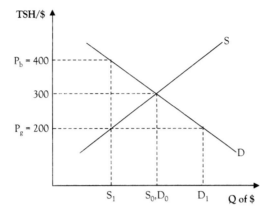

Figure 5.5 Black market for U.S. dollars

Notes: TSH = Tanzanian shillings, P = price, D = demand, S = supply, g = government, b = black market

Government price-fixing is not a sufficient condition for the existence of black markets in foreign exchange. There are two situations where it does not lead to black market activity. The first occurs when the government fixes the price at the market-clearing price. If, in the market depicted in Figure 5.5, the government of Tanzania selects a price of 300 shillings per dollar, all buyers and sellers are accommodated. Hence, there is no economic basis for any black market activity.

If the government fixes the price of foreign exchange at a level which is not a market-clearing one, there need not be black market activity if the government assumes the role of buffer in the market. In this case, the government must be willing and able to accommodate traders by supplying foreign exchange in situations of excess demand, and purchasing foreign exchange when there is excess supply. In Figure 5.5, for example, at the government-determined price (P_g) of 200 shillings per dollar, the government must draw down its foreign exchange reserves in the amount of $D_1 - S_1$. By supplying this amount of foreign exchange to the market, all those demanding foreign exchange are accommodated.

Black markets thrive where government price-fixing results in excess demand for foreign exchange, but the government does not (or cannot) play the role of market buffer. If, at the price of 200 shillings per dollar, the government does not supply foreign exchange to the market, not all traders willing to purchase dollars are able to do so. These excess demand pressures persist even when the government successfully suppresses effective demand through the use of exchange controls and nonconvert-ible currencies. That is, there are still numerous traders who are willing to buy dollars at the prevailing price but are unable to do so because they lack government approval. It is these individuals who are rationed out of the market by exchange controls.

Not only are there dissatisfied buyers in the market, but sellers, too, have reason to be disgruntled. Note that in Figure 5.5, the quantity of dollars S_1 would be demanded at a price of 400 shillings. If everyone complies with foreign exchange laws, sellers receive 200 shillings per dol-lar less than market participants would be willing to pay. Another way of looking at this situation is that sellers are required to pay a tax of 200 shillings per dollar in order to exchange dollars for shillings. This is equivalent to a 50 percent tax rate. More generally, the tax rate (t) is: $t = 1 - (P_g/P_b)$, where P_g is the government price for foreign exchange and P_b is the black market price.

The existence of unsatisfied customers provides a market for the ser-vices of black market traders. What are these traders able to deliver to customers? Sellers receive a higher price for the foreign exchange that they sell. Buyers benefit, too, because the supply of foreign exchange poten-tially is greater and the source is more reliable.

In Figure 5.5, if all sellers of dollars do so in the black market, the extra proceeds available are equal to 200 shillings per dollar times the quantity of dollars sold: $[(P_b - P_g)(S_1)]$. The reward for selling in the black market, which can be substantial, varies directly with the spread between the black market price and the government decreed price. In this case, sellers obtain two times as many shillings per dollar as they would had they sold to the government.

With black market activity, it is possible that the quantity of foreign exchange available may exceed S_1. Higher prices available in the black market provide an incentive to increase the total supply of foreign exchange. If this happens, the result is a movement up the supply curve in Figure 5.5. With greater availability, more buyers of foreign exchange are accommodated. Moreover, excess demand pressures are reduced.

Apart from potentially boosting supply, black markets often offer buyers a more dependable source of supply. Given an excess demand for foreign exchange, buyers relying on government as their source of supply do not always obtain needed foreign exchange. This creates difficulties because many businesses are predicated on a continuous supply of foreign exchange. Some need imported machinery or spare parts in order to operate. Others rely on imported goods for redistribution at the retail level. Because their livelihood depends on satisfying customers, the black market provides an attractive option. Purchasers willing to pay the black market price generally are able to secure a steady source of foreign exchange.

The allocative role played by black markets is illustrated in Figure 5.5. Assume that black market activity does not increase the supply of foreign exchange, and that all available dollars (S_1) are sold at the black market price of 400 shillings. Market disequilibrium, due to government price-fixing, is eliminated through the process of price rationing. Available supply is distributed to relatively high value users. All buyers willing to pay the black market price (P_b) obtain access to foreign exchange that often was unavailable when they attempted to purchase from the government.

Governments respond unfavorably to black market activities, and understandably so. For, their net effect is to reallocate foreign exchange away from the government and to the private sector. Hence, it is not uncommon for governmental officials to use terminology such as corrupt, greedy, and profiteers to describe the activity of these black market traders. In defense of the traders, it is important to remember the source of the area $[(P_b - P_g)(S_1)]$ in Figure 5.5. It does not exist because of black market activity. Rather, it is the result of price distortions brought about by government price-fixing.

If all S_1 dollars are sold to the government at the official price of 200 shillings, and none are sold in the black market, the problem of price distortion still exists. The government now has the same problem that originally confronted suppliers of dollars to the market. It acquired dollars at a price of 200 shillings, but the market value of those dollars is 400 shillings.

The government has two options. First, it can sell all S_1 dollars at the official price of 200 shillings. (After all, this is the official price!) Those buying from the government at this price are, indeed, very fortunate individuals. They are paying only one-half of the market value for the dollars they acquire. If they use these dollars to buy imported goods, the government is, in effect, subsidizing those purchases. If they choose not to buy imports, the minute they walk out of the bank they are able to sell their newly acquired dollars (in the black market) for two times their purchase price. In either case, it is a gift.

A second possibility is that government officials allocating the dollars accept bribes for these dollars. There are not enough dollars to satisfy existing demand at the official price, and buyers are willing to pay more. Given current demand, all S_1 dollars could be sold at a price of 400 shillings. In other words, the area $[(P_b - P_g)(S_1)]$ originally available to those supplying dollars to the market is still there for government officials to exploit. If government officials sell all S_1 dollars for 400 shillings per dollar, and record those transactions at the official price of 200 shillings, the area $[(P_b - P_g)(S_1)]$ now represents total bribery income accruing to those officials.

As noted earlier, exchange controls and nonconvertible currencies impose costs by reducing economic freedom and living standards. Although black market traders provide valuable services to buyers and sellers of foreign exchange, their services are not without cost. Resources employed in these activities could have been used in alternative productive endeavors. The loss of this potential output represents yet a further reduction in living standards as a consequence of the government decision to fix the price of foreign exchange.

CHAPTER 6

Foreign Exchange Markets With Fiat Money: Flexible Exchange Rates

Fiat Money and Flexible Exchange Rates

With flexible exchange rates, market traders buy and sell foreign exchange at any price they find mutually agreeable. From a historical perspective, the world has limited experience with this exchange rate regime. Most countries with relatively high living standards, however, have employed flexible exchange rates since the early 1970s. Although a smaller portion of less developed countries operate with flexible exchange rates, their numbers have increased markedly following the collapse of socialist economies in the 1990s.

Short-Run Exchange Rate Determination

Analysis of price determination in markets with flexible exchange rates differs little from the analysis of other flexible-price markets. Underlying conditions of supply and demand determine market price. When these conditions change, so does market price. Factors affecting quantities of foreign exchange demanded and supplied appear as independent (or right-hand side) variables in demand and supply functions (6.1) and (6.2), respectively.

$$D = f(ER, P_d, P_f, i_d, i_f, v) \qquad (6.1)$$

$$S = f(ER, P_d, P_f, i_d, i_f, u) \qquad (6.2)$$

where ER is the foreign exchange rate (the number of units of domestic
  money per unit of foreign money);

P_d the domestic price level;

P_f the foreign price level;

i_d the domestic interest rate;

i_f the foreign interest rate;

v is a variable capturing all other factors affecting the quantity
  demanded,

and, u is a variable capturing all other factors affecting the quantity
  supplied.

The quantity demanded of foreign exchange depends on a number of
factors. Quantity demanded (D) and the exchange rate (ER), for example,
are inversely related. As the exchange rate declines, foreign goods become
less expensive and the quantity demanded of foreign exchange increases.
Changes in the prices of goods and services, likewise, affect the demand
of foreign exchange. An increase in domestic prices (P_d), with all other
things being equal, increases the demand for foreign goods and, hence,
the demand for foreign exchange. In this case, the relationship between
D and P_d is direct. For foreign prices (P_f), however, the relationship is
indirect. Higher foreign prices make domestic goods more attractive, and
reduce the demand for foreign exchange.

Higher domestic interest rates (i_d) reduce the demand for foreign
exchange; higher foreign interest rates (i_f) increase the demand. These rela-
tionships result from the sensitivity of savers to relative rates of return on
financial instruments. The higher the return on domestic securities (i_d), with
all other things being equal, the lower the demand for foreign exchange
to purchase foreign financial instruments. On the other hand, a higher
return on foreign securities (i_f), with the return on domestic securities held
constant, increases the demand for foreign securities. Increased demand
for foreign securities implies a greater demand for foreign exchange.

Demand function (6.1) is a multidimensional relationship. For
graphical expositions, the two-dimensional demand schedule is preferred.
It is a locus of points showing the quantity of foreign exchange demanded
at each exchange rate, *ceteris paribus*. The demand schedule is derived from
a demand function in the following manner. Hold all independent variables
other than the exchange rate constant. Vary the exchange rate, and trace out
the relationship between the quantity demanded and the exchange rate.

The supply side of the market is developed analogously. Those supplying foreign exchange are demanding domestic money. They are doing so to purchase domestic goods and services and financial instruments. The quantity of foreign exchange supplied (S) is positively related to the exchange rate. A higher exchange rate, with all other things being equal, means that prices of domestic goods are less expensive to foreigners. As they respond by purchasing more domestically produced goods, the quantity supplied of foreign exchange increases. Changes in relative price levels, likewise, affect the supply of foreign exchange. As domestic prices increase, with foreign prices held constant, domestic goods become less price-competitive, and the supply of foreign exchange falls. The opposite, an increase in the supply of foreign exchange, occurs when foreign prices increase relative to domestic prices.

Relative interest rates also affect the supply of foreign exchange. Higher domestic interest rates increase the supply of foreign exchange because foreigners now find domestic financial instruments more attractive. Higher foreign interest rates, on the other hand, reduce the supply of foreign exchange. In this case, more foreigners opt for securities issued in their own countries at the expense of securities issued elsewhere.

Following the approach used when analyzing demand, a *ceteris paribus* assumption is employed to extract the supply schedule (or curve) which is nested in the supply function. One must hold the values of all independent variables other than the exchange rate constant. Tracing out the resulting locus of points representing the quantity of foreign exchange supplied at each exchange rate yields the supply schedule.

Price determination in the market involves the interaction of buyers and sellers of foreign exchange. Their activities are depicted graphically in the demand and supply schedules in Figure 6.1. Equilibrium price, or the market clearing exchange rate, is ER_0. At this price, the quantity of foreign exchange willingly supplied (S_0) is exactly equal to the quantity willingly demanded (D_0).

At any other price, the market is in disequilibrium. At exchange rate ER_1, there is excess demand ($D_1 - S_1$) for foreign exchange. Not all buyers are able to obtain foreign exchange at this price, and competition among them forces the exchange rate upward. The opposite adjustment occurs at price ER_2. Here, there is excess supply of foreign exchange ($S_2 - D_2$) and competition among sellers forces the price downward. By adjusting

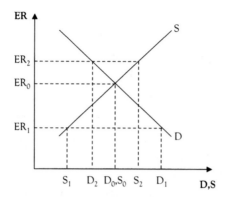

Figure 6.1 Foreign exchange market

Notes: D = demand, S = supply

to clear the market, exchange rates play a critical rationing role in foreign exchange markets.

The gravitation of market price toward its equilibrium level does not imply a stationary foreign exchange rate. In open markets, exchange rates change continuously because underlying market conditions are subject to continuous variation. With varying market conditions, price changes are necessary if the market is to coordinate the diverse plans of multitudes of traders.

From an analytical standpoint, changes in market conditions are captured by relaxing the *ceteris paribus* assumption. This occurs with any change in a right-hand side variable other than ER in Equations 6.1 or 6.2. If the variable is in the demand function, the result is a shift in the demand schedule. For a change in a variable in the supply function, it is the supply schedule that shifts. Both schedules shift when a variable that appears in both functions changes. To facilitate understanding, it is customary to change one independent variable at a time and to examine the implications of that change.

Domestic prices (P_d) are positively related to the demand for foreign exchange (Equation 6.1) and negatively related to the supply (Equation 6.2). Hence, an increase in the domestic price level causes the demand curve to shift to the right and the supply schedule to shift to the left. At the previously prevailing exchange rate (ER_0), there now is excess demand for foreign exchange. Competition among buyers forces the price of foreign exchange higher, that is, foreign money appreciates in value relative to domestic money. This situation is shown in Figure 6.2a, where the new equilibrium price is ER_1. Had the domestic price level fallen, instead, domestic goods would become more competitive in international markets. Domestic money would have appreciated in value on the foreign exchange market.

Changes in foreign prices (P_f) also affect relative prices and the exchange rate. The demand for foreign exchange is negatively related to the foreign price level; the supply of foreign exchange is positively related. An increase in foreign prices (all other things being equal) causes the demand curve for foreign exchange to shift to the left and the supply

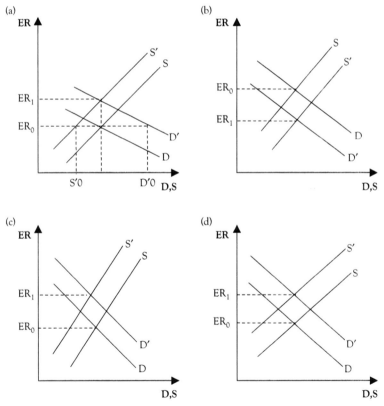

Figure 6.2 Foreign exchange market with parametric changes:
(a) increase in domestic price level; (b) increase in foreign price level;
(c) decrease in domestic interest rates; and (d) increase in foreign interest rates

Notes: D = demand, S = supply

curve to shift to the right (Figure 6.2b). As a consequence, the equilibrium exchange rate falls from ER_0 to ER_1. Domestic money appreciates in value in the foreign exchange market or, equivalently, foreign exchange depreciates in value. The opposite occurs when foreign prices fall.

Changing capital flows, likewise, affect exchange rates. Movements in relative interest rate levels are hypothesized to induce such changes. A fall in the domestic interest rate (all other things being equal), for example, makes domestic securities less competitive in global financial markets. Although their level remains unchanged, foreign interest rates now are more attractive. The result is an increased demand for foreign exchange, a reduced supply, and a higher foreign exchange rate (Figure 6.2c). These observed shifts in demand and supply curves are consistent with Equations 6.1 and 6.2, where the demand for foreign exchange is inversely related to domestic interest rates and the supply is directly related.

Movements in foreign interest rates affect exchange rates for the same reason, that is, investors are sensitive to relative rates of return. The quantity of foreign exchange demanded is directly related to foreign interest rates; the quantity supplied is inversely related. A rise in foreign interest rates increases the relative attractiveness of foreign securities. The demand curve for foreign exchange shifts to the right and the supply curve to the left (Figure 6.2d). Foreign exchange appreciates in value (or domestic money falls in value). Falling foreign interest rates have the opposite effect.

In summary, when markets are open and traders are free to establish mutually agreeable prices, prices tend to vary continuously because underlying market conditions constantly change. Open markets in foreign exchange conform to this pattern, that is, exchange rates exhibit continual variation. Two important factors responsible for short-run variation in exchange rates are movements in relative prices and interest rates.

The Dirty Float

In countries where exchange rates are free to vary, it is not always true that market forces, alone, determine exchange rates. Occasionally, central banks enter foreign exchange markets and buy and sell currencies to affect market price. This is referred to as central bank intervention in foreign exchange markets. When it occurs, observed exchange rates are not strictly the result of market forces, but reflect these activities as well. The term dirty float is an acknowledgement that central banks do, at times, play this role.

When central banks intervene in foreign exchange markets, they can do so individually or collectively. Recently, collective intervention has been popular. A group of industrial countries known as the G7 are loosely organized for that purpose.[1] Those countries normally justify their collective action as an effort to coordinate macroeconomic policies across countries. Hence, their joint actions frequently are called policy coordination.

It is doubtful, however, that G7 countries have either the ability or willingness to successfully coordinate macroeconomic policies. To date, such efforts mainly have taken the form of joint purchases or sales of U.S. dollars—the principal international medium of exchange. The objective has been to bring about a foreign-exchange market price for the U.S. dollar that is different from how market traders would value the dollar.

When the dollar is falling, for example, central banks may agree to purchase dollars to keep it from falling further. An intervention of this type is illustrated in Figure 6.3, which shows the market for U.S. dollars in terms of Japanese Yen (¥). At the current rate of exchange, $(¥/\$)_0$, there is an excess supply of dollars in the market. If market forces are allowed to operate, the price of the dollar will depreciate to the level $(¥/\$)_1$. To keep

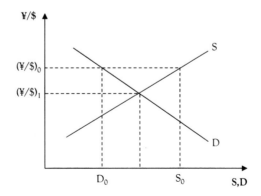

Figure 6.3 Market for U.S. dollars

Notes: ¥ = Japanese yen, D = demand, S = supply

Exhibit 6.1

Balance sheet changes with intervention

Federal Reserve Bank		foreign exchange dealer	
¥	–	¥	+
$	+	$	–

this from happening, central banks must intervene by purchasing dollars in the amount of $(S_0 - D_0)$. These purchases increase the demand for dollars, and the quantity demanded is now exactly equal to the supplied (S_0). Intervention, in this case, keeps the dollar from falling.

The effects of these transactions on the balance sheets of participants are shown in Exhibit 6.1. For simplicity purposes, only balance sheets for the intervening central bank (the United States Federal Reserve Bank) and a single trader (foreign exchange dealer) are shown. The Federal Reserve's balance sheet shows an increase in the holding of dollar balances that it acquired by selling yen. This represents a loss of foreign exchange reserves for the U.S. central bank. The private trader (foreign exchange dealer), on the other hand, shows an increase in holdings of yen obtained by selling dollars to the Federal Reserve Bank.

While central banks can temporarily affect the exchange rate, it is much more difficult in the long run. This is not surprising because such interventions are an attempt to override market outcomes.[2] Unless market conditions change, short-term interventions only delay the movement of an exchange rate. If market conditions do change, they may well change in a manner that pushes the exchange rate in a direction opposite to that preferred by the central banks. More intervention now is required and further erosion of central bank reserves occurs. The continuing loss of foreign exchange reserves is a major factor militating against longer-term intervention by central banks.[3]

Policy ineffectiveness does not imply that central bank interventions are without effect. By diverting focus away from economic considerations, they politicize activity in foreign exchange markets. Pressure groups representing special interests now know where to go if market price moves unfavorably for them. In addition, central bank interventions often result in a transfer of wealth from central banks to private traders. This occurs, for example, when the exchange rate in Figure 6.3 eventually falls to its equilibrium level (¥/$)$_1$. As seen in Exhibit 6.1, the wealth position of the Federal Reserve Bank has deteriorated because it accumulated assets that fell in value ($) and disposed of assets that subsequently appreciated in value (¥). Foreign exchange dealers are the beneficiaries. They accumulated yen-denominated assets that gained value and disposed of U.S. dollar-denominated assets that subsequently depreciated.

Long-Run Exchange Rate Determination: Purchasing Power Parity

The law of one price is the proposition that an identical commodity should sell for the same price without regard to its location.[4] Market activity insures this outcome because profit opportunities exist whenever the same object sells for two different prices. Traders obtain profit by purchasing in the relatively low-price market and selling in the relatively high-price market. Increasing demand in the relatively low-price market and increasing supply in the relatively high-price market results in price convergence and, eventually, a uniform market price. This trading activity is called arbitrage; those practicing it, arbitrageurs.

The purchasing power parity (PPP) theory of exchange rates applies the law of one price to money. Money should only have one price, that is, it should have PPP (or equality). In this context, money is not used as a unit of account. The reason is that the exchange value (or price) of a unit of money in terms of itself is always one. Rather, the price of money refers to how money exchanges relative to all other goods and services. The relationship is inverse, as is indicated in Equation 6.3. An increase in the average price of goods and services (P) is the same thing as a reduction in the purchasing power of money (PPM), or its price. Conversely, with a decrease in the average price, a unit of money will purchase more.

$$PPM = 1/P, \qquad (6.3)$$

where PPM is the purchasing power of money, or its price, and P is the average price for goods and services.

In the international economy, a unit of money has a single price if it purchases an equivalent amount of goods and services in each country. If it does not, money has more than one price, and profit opportunities exist. This stimulates arbitrage activity, which causes exchange rates to move in a manner that brings about purchasing power parity.

Consider the following example involving two countries: Mexico and the United States. Rather than considering all goods and services, a simplifying assumption is made. There is only one good, shoes, that are identical in both countries. The shoes sell for $50 in the United States, and 500 pesos in Mexico. The current exchange rate is one U.S. dollar for 10 Mexican pesos.

At that exchange rate, PPP exists for both currencies. Individuals in the United States can purchase the shoes in their own country for $50. Alternately, they can exchange $50 for 500 pesos in the foreign exchange market, and purchase the same shoes in Mexico for 500 pesos. One U.S. dollar exchanges for 1/50th of a pair of shoes in both countries, that is, the dollar has PPP.

For citizens of Mexico, shoes purchased domestically cost 500 pesos. 500 pesos will exchange for $50 in the foreign exchange market, which is exactly the price of that pair of shoes in the United States. One Mexican peso exchanges for 1/500th of a pair of shoes in both countries, and the Mexican peso also has PPP.

Now, assume that these two countries follow radically different monetary policies. In the United States, the money supply does not change, while the Bank of Mexico increases the money supply in that country at the rate of 50 percent per annum. Furthermore, assume that prices (including the price of shoes) mirror money growth in the two countries. That is, the average price of goods and services remains the same in the United States, but increases at the annual rate of 50 percent in Mexico. After one year, the price of shoes remains at $50 in the United States, but increases to 750 pesos in Mexico.

At the previously prevailing exchange rate, neither currency now has PPP. One U.S. dollar exchanges for 1/50th of a pair of shoes in the United States, but only 1/75th of a pair of shoes in Mexico. Likewise, one peso now exchanges for 1/750th of a pair of shoes in Mexico, but 1/500th of a pair of shoes in the United States.

This departure from PPP gives rise to arbitrage activity in money. The arbitrageurs, in this case, are consumers. Both currencies have a higher price, or exchange value, in the United States. That is, each will purchase a larger quantity of goods in that country. With consumers in both countries preferring to purchase goods in the United States, Mexico now experiences a balance of payments deficit (and the United States, a surplus).

With flexible exchange rates, the value of the Mexican peso will fall (in relation to the dollar) on the foreign exchange market. That is, the peso depreciates in value; the dollar appreciates. Exchange rate adjustment continues until the foreign exchange market clears.

In this example, market clearing occurs at the exchange rate: 15 pesos = $1. At this exchange rate, both monies again have PPP. The dollar purchases 1/50th of a pair of shoes both in the United States and in Mexico. The Mexican peso will purchase 1/750th of a pair in each country. There is no source for further disturbance in the exchange rate.

The adjustment process just described illustrates the PPP theory of exchange rates. According to the theory, long-run changes in exchange rates occur to bring about PPP for each currency involved. Note that the use of the term parity does not mean that both currencies exchange for the same amount of goods and services. Clearly, in the previous example, one U.S. dollar purchases more goods and services than does the Mexican peso.

With PPP, changes in exchange rates result from differences in price-level changes for individual countries. These differences lead to a deviation from PPP. Restoration of PPP occurs through arbitrage activity in money (and, thus, goods). Money moves from markets where its value is relatively low, to markets where it has a relatively high value. Exchange rates adjust until the monies involved have PPP, and the law of one price again applies to money.

The PPP theory has assumed elevated importance in the world of fiat money. Individual countries have monetary autonomy, that is, they have the freedom to increase (or decrease) the money supply at their own discretion. Under this monetary arrangement, individual countries have increased the money supply at widely varying rates. The result has been great variation in inflation rates from country to country.

Foreign exchange markets, through variation in exchange rates, accommodate these differences in monetary policies. Countries with relatively rapid money growth (and inflation) experience depreciation in their exchange rate. Those with more conservative monetary policies (and lower inflation) generally experience appreciation.

CHAPTER 7

Proposals Advanced by Critics of Flexible Exchange Rates

Analysis in this book has focused on how foreign exchange markets work. From an analytical standpoint, individual exchange rate regimes generally cannot be separated from an underlying monetary standard. Four different exchange rate regimes and associated monetary standards have been discussed.

1. Foreign exchange markets with commodity money.
2. Foreign exchange markets with fiduciary money.
3. Foreign exchange markets with fiat money: fixed exchange rates.
4. Foreign exchange markets with fiat money: flexible exchange rates.

We currently live in a world of fiat money. For the United States, use of this type of money is a relatively new phenomenon. It dates from 1933 when it was imposed upon the country during the Franklin D. Roosevelt administration. Given our limited experience with this form of money, the institutional arrangements surrounding our foreign exchange markets are also relatively new.

During the 80-year U.S. experiment with fiat money, both exchange rate regimes (3) and (4) were employed, and each for nearly an equivalent amount of time. For (approximately) the first half of the period, the United States had fixed exchange rates; the second half, flexible exchange rates. Many other countries, influenced by the dominant position of the United States in the world economy, followed U.S. leadership and, consequently, shared this roughly 40/40-year pattern of exchange rate regimes.

Many familiar with our current exchange rate regime may be satisfied with how it is functioning. That sentiment is not shared by all. Four decades of accumulated experience is ample time for market participants to discover things they consider unsatisfactory with any set of market institutions, and that includes foreign exchange markets with flexible exchange rates. For some, the dissatisfaction is sufficient to call for a change in exchange rate regimes. While they appear to be in the minority at present, that may not always be the case. Thus, it is worthwhile to examine the alternatives proposed by these critics of flexible exchange rates.

While their proposals are dissimilar, critics generally are thinking regressively in the following sense. They favor returning to either exchange rate regime (2) or exchange rate regime (3). This is not unimportant. It means that we know something about what their proposed changes portend. Analyses in Chapters 4 and 5 are useful in assessing the likely consequences of those changes and, in addition, there are available empirics. We have prior experience with these exchange rate regimes.

Fiduciary Money Standard

Many economists in the Austrian tradition favor a return to the gold standard, or replacing fiat money with fiduciary money that is fully convertible into gold. This monetary standard has fixed exchange rates: regime (2). Currently, the prospect for such a change seems remote. However, it cannot be dismissed as out of the question.[1] The prospect for a return to the gold standard improves dramatically in the wake of a monetary crisis, something that cannot be precluded in a world of fiat money.

Most monetary crises under a fiat money regime involve hyperinflation. Because government is the source of hyperinflation, bringing hyperinflation to a halt invariably requires government action. The question becomes one of how to move forward. To date, in virtually all cases, governments have opted to return to a renewed fiat money standard. If hyperinflation were to occur in the United Sates, the outcome could be different because of the U.S. leadership role in the world economy. A possible alternative, in this situation, is a return to some form of fiduciary money standard such as the gold standard.

We know from Chapter 4 some of the basic features of the gold standard (and fiduciary money standards more generally). Exchange rates are fixed, but not because of government price-fixing. In this case, the fixed exchange rates are the result of actions undertaken by market traders.[2] Exchanges are made at a price that reflects differences in the commodity content of the two monies involved. Any deviation from this fixed exchange rate means that a given amount of the underlying commodity (embodied in one of the monies) is exchanging for a different amount of the same commodity (embodied in the second money). Arbitrage activities correct any such temporary deviation from the law of one price.

A second feature of the gold standard is that there are no balance of payments (BOP) crises.[3] BOP crises arise when countries experience chronic BOP deficits financed by shipping domestic money overseas. Repatriating that money back into the country at the central bank level reduces the foreign exchange reserves of a central bank. A BOP crisis occurs when those reserves approach zero in the limit.

That is not possible under a gold standard because repeated BOP deficits tend not to occur. BOP disequilibria are self-correcting via the Hume price-specie flow mechanism. Money flows from BOP deficit countries to surplus countries and drives the BOP position toward zero. Eventually, the foreign exchange market clears at the same fixed exchange rate.

Third, the monetary role of the central bank is greatly diminished under the gold standard. Money growth is largely constrained by the discovery and extraction of new sources of gold. Moreover, many changes in the money supply are brought about by BOP disequilibria, as gold is shipped from deficit countries to surplus countries. The fiduciary component of the money supply is also limited by the convertibility option. Continued printing of fiduciary money to offset gold outflows eventually destabilizes the financial system. These multiple impediments to monetary control contrast sharply with the considerable monetary autonomy exercised by central banks under the fiat money standard.

Many economists have reservations about sacrificing such government control over money. That is especially true of economists steeped in the Keynesian tradition. The major motivation for leaving the gold standard was to give government greater control over money. Restoring the gold standard means relinquishing that government control over money.

A final outcome associated with a return to fiduciary money is less contentious. Much greater long-run price stability is a virtual certainty. Economic analysis reveals how market forces tend to bring this about. Our past experience with fiduciary money provides further support for this proposition. As shown in Figure 2.1 (Chapter 2), the average price of goods and services when the United States left gold standard was not much different than it was in 1780 (during the Revolutionary War). Compare this with changes in the value of fiat money in the United States under the watch of the Federal Reserve. Since the imposition of fiat money in 1933, the U.S. dollar has lost approximately 94 percent of its purchasing power (relative to goods and services).

Money with a relatively stable purchasing power yields significant benefits. Some of these benefits have been sacrificed with the use of fiat money. One is that market prices better serve as a conduit for transferring information, something that Friedrich Hayek emphasized in a classic paper on how markets utilize information.[4] With fiat money inflation, some of the informational content of prices is destroyed. The result is impaired decision making and the likelihood of a less effective use of available resources.

Money with a stable value also provides a greater flow of services to users of money. One such service is the store of value function of money, a service that has been largely decimated by the central banks of the world. If the purchasing power of money is stabilized, money will again compete more effectively with real assets and stocks and bonds as a vehicle for transferring wealth through time.

The service of money as a medium of exchange, in many instances, has also been diminished with adoption of fiat money. That is particularly true for countries that have experienced hyperinflation. In this situation, users of money frequently resort to barter or engage in money substitution. The latter occurs when individuals substitute the money of another country for the money of their own country.

One might correctly observe that hyperinflation has not afflicted the United States. While that is true, we probably share a modicum of responsibility for the hyperinflation that occurs elsewhere. The United

States is the dominant economic power of the world. With most other countries assuming a subsidiary role, it is very practical, if not essential, for them to mimic our monetary behavior. That means using fiat money if that is our choice of a monetary standard. It is the fiat money standard that makes hyperinflation possible.

Fixed Exchange Rates With Fiat Money: Government Price-Fixing in Foreign Exchange Markets

A more likely prospect for eliminating our current exchange rate regime is to retain fiat money but return to government price-fixing of exchange rates: regime (3). If this were to mimic our previous experience, governments would price each individual currency in terms of gold. This results in a fixed exchange rate for each pair of currencies. This arrangement gives the appearance that countries are returning to some form of gold standard. That decidedly is not the case. To emphasize that this is not so, Milton Friedman referred to this type of arrangement as a pseudo gold standard.[5]

The motivation for returning to government price-fixing in foreign exchange markets is disenchantment with the continuous exchange rate changes that occur in the world of flexible exchange rates. These changes expose market participants to foreign exchange risk, a risk that can affect the outcomes of international transactions. The argument is that this risk largely is eliminated when exchange rates are fixed.

This argument is flawed. There is no assurance that foreign exchange risk will vanish with government price-fixing in foreign exchange markets, especially in the long run. Our experience with fixed exchange rates under the Bretton Woods agreement validates this point. There were numerous cases where exchange rates changed, and sometimes significantly. France devalued the franc.[6] Great Britain devalued the pound, and the United States devalued the dollar when it jettisoned the adjustable peg system in 1971. Many less developed countries also devalued their currencies, some of them more than one time.

These experiences document the existence of foreign exchange risk in a world of fiat money with government price-fixing in foreign exchange markets. In some instances, the risk may be elevated. That can occur if more gradual changes in exchange rates (under a flexible exchange rate regime) are replaced with quantum shifts in exchange rates that occur when government reprices foreign exchange.[7] A devaluation, which can result in an instantaneous change of 10 or 20 percent in an exchange rate, exposes traders to substantial foreign exchange risk.

The fundamental problem with government price-fixing in foreign exchange markets is no different from government price-fixing in any market. Market prices are a manifestation of subjective valuations by market traders. There is no reason to believe that the price set by government will match the valuations of market traders. Where discrepancies occur, market participants respond in a manner that is amenable to analysis, something undertaken in Chapter 5. As a consequence, we have foreknowledge of likely outcomes with government price-fixing in foreign exchange markets. A partial litany follows.

First, fixed exchange rate systems (with fiat money) are potentially unstable. There are periodic BOP crises. That occurs when countries experience persistent BOP deficits. Those deficits are financed by shipping domestic money balances abroad. That money is most often repatriated back into the country at the central bank level. Repatriation by the central bank reduces the foreign exchange reserves of the central bank. The lower limit on those reserves is zero. When that limit is approached, the country experiences a BOP crisis. Crises of this sort are a direct result of government price-fixing in foreign exchange markets.

Second, black markets in foreign exchange appear. Market traders often find that transacting business at the government-determined exchange rate gives them an unfavorable price or an unreliable source of supply. An individual bringing foreign exchange into the country, for example, often discovers that trading at the official exchange rate involves selling at a price significantly below market value. The difference between the official exchange rate and the market value is an implicit tax. This tax can be substantial, in some cases in excess of 75 percent.

At the same time, an automobile dealer who must have a reliable source of foreign exchange (to import autos) encounters difficulties because of the chronic shortage of foreign exchange in the country. The risk of not obtaining foreign exchange can elevate when the government is in charge of allocating available foreign exchange. When the individual bringing foreign exchange into the country and the automobile dealer find one another, it is a match made in heaven. Black markets in foreign exchange are all about rectifying a dysfunctional market occasioned by government mispricing of foreign exchange. Black market traders are able to undo some of the damage inflicted by the mispricing.

Third, in countries experiencing BOP deficits, governments frequently enact policies that cause living standards to fall. They do so to deflect pressures they feel as a result those payments deficits. The underlying premise is that it is possible to significantly reduce (or possibly eliminate) such deficits by passing laws. In some instances, and for short periods, they can diminish the size of the deficit. It is possible to reduce the demand for foreign exchange by implementing tariffs and quotas. Exchange controls by government can further limit the effective demand for foreign exchange.

The problem is that such policies are a classic case of treating the symptom rather than the cause. Moreover, they often do great harm. Restricting trade flows in this manner means sacrificing the potential gains from trade. When that happens, living standards are adversely affected. Previous episodes indicate that countries most likely to enact restrictive policies with a vengeance were the less developed countries of the world. This meant that some of the world's poorest people were made to suffer to maintain a system of government-determined prices in foreign exchange markets.

For the present, neither the gold standard nor fixed exchange rates established by governments (under our current fiat money standard) seem likely to replace the current system of flexible exchange rates. It is foolish to discount them entirely, however. What drives many significant shifts in institutional arrangements are social and economic turmoil. In a world of fiat money, very high rates of inflation or even hyperinflation have the potential to cause such turmoil.

Notes

Chapter 1

1. Gerdes (1997).
2. Gerdes (2014).
3. Friedman (1968).
4. Steil (2013).
5. Husted and Melvin (2013).
6. Two are Rhodes (1993) and Barton et al. (2006).
7. Melvin and Norrbin (2012); Moffett et al. (2011).

Chapter 2

1. For a more detailed analysis of money, banking, and monetary policy, see Gerdes (2014).
2. It is not uncommon for individuals to reject the money of a government. Examples are reversions to barter and cases of money substitution, where individuals reject the money of their country (when making exchanges) in favor of the money of another country. Dollarization in Mexico is an example of the latter.
3. For an extended version of this discussion of monetary systems, see Gerdes (1997).
4. It is erroneous to assert, as some economists do, that fiat money has no intrinsic value. From this perspective, the marginal subjective value of fiat money, when used for nonmonetary purposes, is zero. We know that is not the case. Using stacks of fiat money as a doorstop, a paperweight, or as kindling in the fireplace all have potential value for the consumer. The reason we do not generally observe these activities is the inequality expressed in the first property of fiat money. Money tends to have greater value when used as money than when used for nonmonetary purposes.
5. Had consumers preferred fiat money, issuers of fiduciary money would have voluntarily accommodated those preferences.
6. Some make the case that the U.S. government did not leave the gold standard until August 15, 1971. On that date, President Richard Nixon closed the U.S. gold window to all foreign central banks. From 1933 to 1971, gold did have a very limited monetary role. Governments allowed central banks to settle imbalances of payments through gold shipments. Nixon's action eliminated this option. It makes little sense, however, to maintain that the United States

was on the gold standard from 1933 to 1971 when it was illegal for all households and all private businesses in the United States to possess monetary gold.

7. Deflation is also self-limiting with fiduciary money. Market forces tend to increase the quantity of commodity money. If government reduces the quantity of fiduciary money to offset this, the ratio of fiduciary money to commodity money falls. The lower limit for this ratio is zero. When the ratio approaches zero, government is no longer able to offset the rising production of commodity money. Increases in the total quantity of money eventually bring the deflation to an end.

Chapter 3

1. There is a more generic use of the term exchange rate. Whenever an exchange occurs, the number of units of one item that exchanges for a single unit of the other is referred to as an exchange rate. In the context of international financial markets, the term exchange rate assumes a much more specialized meaning.

2. We are abstracting from unilateral transfers. Some countries are recipients of foreign aid, which enables them (in the aggregate) to purchase more than they sell.

3. When we say that a country financed its BOT surplus by importing financial instruments, we are not suggesting that the country made a conscious decision to be a net importer of financial instruments. The basic decision-making units are individual economic agents, and the BOP accounting system under consideration is a consolidation of the transactions made by these units. In a money economy, one side of every transaction is money. When we sum international transactions across economic agents, if they sell more G and NM than they buy, by definition they will be importing money balances in the aggregate.

Chapter 4

1. In practice, gold points about this 2:1 mint par rate of exchange provided a trading range within which the price of gold could fluctuate without inducing arbitrage activity. These gold points reflected the costs of shipping gold from one market to another.

2. This part of Hume's argument is in the quantity theory of money tradition.

3. A surplus country can sterilize money inflows by reducing the quantity of fiduciary money to offset specie inflows. The ratio of commodity money to fiduciary money (G_M/FG_M) in the country increases. Convertibility is not

jeopardized. When surplus countries behave in this manner, a greater portion of the adjustment necessary to restore BOP equilibrium must occur in the deficit country. With perfect sterilization, all of the adjustment occurs in the deficit country

Chapter 5

1. For further discussion of nonconvertible currencies, refer to the section on nonconvertible currencies on pp. 54–58.
2. Austrian economists in this tradition include Ludwig von Mises, Gottfried Haberler, and Friedrich A. Hayek.
3. Friedman (1961).
4. As a condition of membership, each member country of the IMF was required to subscribe a quota of gold and its domestic currency to the IMF. The gold and currencies so accumulated by the IMF were used to make loans to individual countries.
5. In addition to the IMF, another postwar agreement contributed significantly to dismantling of trade barriers. The General Agreement on Tariffs and Trade provided a framework for governments to negotiate reductions in trade barriers.
6. We are abstracting here from transactions costs which, in percentage terms, tend to be quite small for large transactions.
7. It is assumed here that the country also has exhausted its potential for borrowing foreign exchange.
8. When the money issued by foreign governments also is used to make domestic purchases, it is referred to as currency substitution. This has become more prevalent in less developed countries with rapid money growth and a commensurate decline in the purchasing power of their money. Currency substitution is simply a generalization of monetary behavior occurring when countries adopt nonconvertible currencies.

Chapter 6

1. The group of seven consists of the United States, the United Kingdom, Japan, France, Germany, Canada, and Italy.
2. The central banks in question are swimming against the current. Their interventions are an attempt to keep market price from moving in the direction it is heading.
3. The monetary independence of individual countries also is subverted. After all, long-term intervention is simply another name for government price-fixing in foreign exchange markets.

4. Exceptions to the law of one price can occur. Transportation costs serve as a natural barrier, and a price differential reflecting transportation costs can exist without encouraging arbitrage. Government imposed barriers to trade such as tariffs and quotas also can lead to price differences that are not eliminated by arbitrage activity. These are artificial barriers.

Chapter 7

1. Upon personal reflection, in 1980, I would have considered the dissolution of the Soviet Union and the unification of Germany as comparably remote.

2. The assumption is that the major trading countries simultaneously return to the gold standard. If the United States were to unilaterally return to the gold standard, the situation changes in ways that are not developed here. Countries not adopting the gold standard are likely to experience persistent depreciation in their exchange rates given the predilection of central banks in those countries to create fiat money.

3. The following conceptual counterexample is unlikely because of its outcome. The government in a country with a BOP deficit persistently issues fiduciary money to offset the outflow of commodity money. In this case, the BOP deficit is not dissipated via the Hume mechanism. The problem here is that such a monetary policy will eventually lead to a collapse of the country's financial system. Once bank depositors perceive that commercial banks will be unable to honor the convertibility option, they have an incentive to exchange bank deposits for currency. When generalized, this behavior results in a bank run.

4. Hayek (1945).

5. Friedman (1961).

6. Devaluation occurs when a government reduces a fixed exchange rate. Euphemistically speaking, this is a change in the official exchange rate. Often the result is a significant price change that is instantaneous.

7. In unpublished research in the 1980s, I found that a set of countries with flexible exchange rates had greater exchange rate stability than did a second set of countries with fixed exchange rates. The reason was the quantum shifts in exchange rates that were occurring in the latter set of countries. The directional changes in those exchange rates tended to be monotonic.

References

David, P.A. and Solar, P. 1977. "A Bicentenary Contribution to the History of the Cost of Living in America." *Research in Economic History* 2 reprinted in John J. McCusker. 2001. *How Much Is That in Real Money: A Historical Commodity Price Index for Use as a Deflator of Money Values in the Economy of the United States of America*. Worcester, MA: American Antiquarian Society.

Gerdes, W.D. 1997. "A Taxonomies from the Consumer's Perspective." *The Journal of Economics* 23, no. 3, pp. 21–29.

Gerdes, W.D. 2014. *Money and Banking: An Intermediate Market-Based Approach*. New York, NY: Business Expert Press.

Friedman, M. 1968. *Dollars and Deficits: Inflation, Monetary Policy, and the Balance of Payments*. Upper Saddle River, NJ: Prentice-Hall.

Friedman, M. October, 1961. "Real and Pseudo Gold Standards." *The Journal of Law and Economics* 4, pp. 66–79.

Hayek, F.A. September, 1945. "The Use of Knowledge in Society." *American Economic Review* 35, no. 4, pp. 519–30.

Husted, S. and Melvin, M. 2013. *International Economics*. 9th ed. Boston, MA: Pearson Addison-Wesley.

Melvin, M. and Norrbin, S. 2012. *International Money and Finance*. 8th ed. Boston, MA: Pearson Addison-Wesley.

Moffett, M.H., Stonehill, A.I., and Eiteman, D.K. 2011. *Fundamentals of Multinational Finance*. 4th ed. Upper Saddle River, NJ: Pearson Prentice-Hall.

Steil, B. 2013. *The Battle of Bretton Woods: John Maynard Keynes, Harry Dexter White, and the Making of a New World Order*, The Council on Foreign Relations. Princeton, NJ: Princeton University Press.

U.S. Department of Labor. 2014. "Consumer Price Index," *Bureau of Labor Statistics*. www.bls.gov/cpi.

Index

OTHER TITLES FROM THE ECONOMICS COLLECTION

Philip Romero, The University of Oregon and Jeffrey Edwards,
North Carolina A&T State University, Editors

- *Regression for Economics* by Shahdad Naghshpour
- *Statistics for Economics* by Shahdad Naghshpour
- *How Strong Is Your Firm's Competitive Advantage?* by Daniel Marburger
- *A Primer on Microeconomics* by Thomas Beveridge
- *Game Theory: Anticipating Reactions for Winning Actions* by Mark L. Burkey
- *A Primer on Macroeconomics* by Thomas Beveridge
- *Economic Decision Making Using Cost Data: A Guide for Managers* by Daniel Marburger
- *The Fundamentals of Money and Financial Systems* by Shahdad Naghshpour
- *International Economics: Understanding the Forces of Globalization for Managers* by Paul Torelli
- *The Economics of Crime* by Zagros Madjd-Sadjadi
- *Money and Banking: An Intermediate Market-Based Approach* by William D. Gerdes
- *Basel III Liquidity Regulation and Its Implications* by Mark A. Petersen and Janine Mukuddem-Petersen
- *Saving American Manufacturing: The Fight for Jobs, Opportunity, and National Security* by William R. Killingsworth
- *What Hedge Funds Really Do: An Introduction to Portfolio Management* by Philip J. Romero and Tucker Balch
- *Advanced Economies and Emerging Markets: Prospects for Globalization* by Marcus Goncalves, José Alves, Carlos Frota, Harry Xia, and Rajabahadur V. Arcot
- *Comparing Emerging and Advanced Markets: Current Trends and Challenges* by Marcus Goncalves and Harry Xia

Announcing the Business Expert Press Digital Library

*Concise E-books Business Students Need
for Classroom and Research*

This book can also be purchased in an e-book collection by your library as
- a one-time purchase,
- that is owned forever,
- allows for simultaneous readers,
- has no restrictions on printing, and
- can be downloaded as PDFs from within the library community.

Our digital library collections are a great solution to beat the rising cost of textbooks. E-books can be loaded into their course management systems or onto students' e-book readers.

The **Business Expert Press** digital libraries are very affordable, with no obligation to buy in future years. For more information, please visit **www.businessexpertpress.com/librarians**. To set up a trial in the United States, please email **sales@businessexpertpress.com**.

CPSIA information can be obtained at www.ICGtesting.com
Printed in the USA
LVOW10s2138121214

418641LV00010B/161/P